PROJECTS / PROCESSES VOLUME V

Other Everydays

PROJECTS / PROCESSES VOLUME V

Other Everydays

Series Editor: Senjuti Mukherjee

HARPER DESIGN
An Imprint of HarperCollins*Publishers*

First published in India in 2019 by
HarperCollins *Publishers*
A-75, Sector 57, Noida, Uttar Pradesh 201301, India
www.harpercollins.co.in

2 4 6 8 10 9 7 5 3 1

P-ISBN: 978-93-5357-534-2

Typeset in 9/14.2 Freight at
Serendipity Arts Foundation

Printed and bound at
Replika Press Pvt. Ltd.

Contents

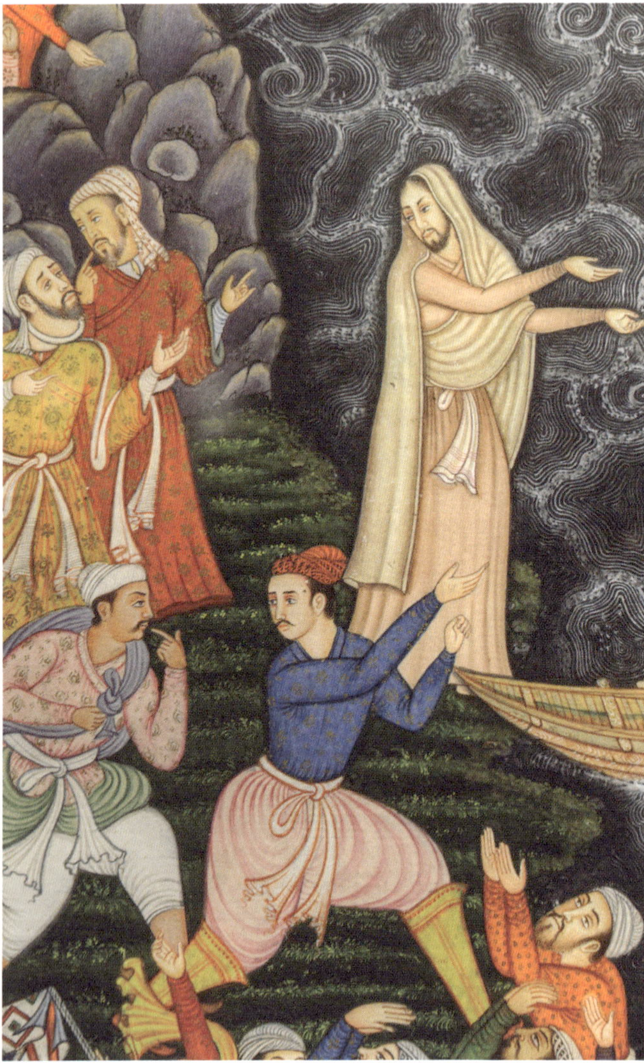

Detail of *Issanama* (2017-2018); Manish Soni; Series of 12; Opaque watercolour and natural pigments on hand-made paper; From the Sarmaya Arts Foundation, Mumbai

The Sacred Everyday: Embracing the Risk of Difference

Curated by Ranjit Hoskote

Venues Adil Shah Palace and Santa Monica Church

Curatorial Note

Collections *Charles Correa Foundation, Goa State Museum, Jyotindra & Jutta Jain Collection, Museum of Christian Art, Phillips Antiques, Sarmaya Collection, Sunaparanta Centre for the Arts and Swaraj Art Archive, Leonard and Naomi Menezes Collection, Goa*
Artists *Ghulam Rasool Santosh, Priya Pereira, Smriti Dixit, Vidya Kamat and Youdhisthir Maharjan*
Curatorial Assistants *Khorshed Deboo, Zoya Kathawala, Priyanka Tagore and Prarthana Tagore*
Special Thanks *TARQ, Blueprint Gallery*
Curator *Ranjit Hoskote*

India's greatest strength, for millennia, has been its dynamic ability to engage with a diversity of sources and impulses, to absorb and transmute them into a syncretic and kaleidoscopic culture. This has also been the greatest strength of the religious imagination in India. Every religion in the subcontinent has been nourished by the confluence of abundantly plural traditions, conversations across the lines of particular idioms of belief and contributions from every stratum of society. At a time when religion has been weaponised into a top-down, authoritarian means of stifling dissent, it is salutary to remember that the religious imagination in India has always been sustained by festive, playful, bottom-up impulses of improvisation. It was never embalmed in the singularity of a canon, but relayed in versions by agents who had a considerable measure of freedom in imagining iconography, creating narratives, improvising new stories and performing new interpretations. This is not high culture. This is not academic theorising. This is the extraordinary character of the ordinary experience of a multi-layered, multidimensional, constantly self-transfiguring culture. This is the reality to which *The Sacred Everyday* bears witness.

The Sacred Everyday shows how various belief systems have intersected and incorporated one another's imagery and practices. Religions dissimilar or seemingly opposed at the level of doctrine have come to share, with confidence, elements of iconography, ritual and mythic narrative. *The Sacred Everyday* upholds this history, not as a fossil heritage but as an integral element of the Subcontinent's lived experience, even in the face of a tendency towards religious polarisation and the creation of hard-edged, mutually exclusionary cultural identities. This explains our subtitle here: Embracing the *Risk of Difference*.

This exhibition explored the interrelationship between the sacred—the domain of the divine, iconic, cosmic and sublime—on one hand, and the everyday—the realm of the human, intimate, individual and domestic—on the other. This interrelationship was articulated through ritual and festivity, the robustly vernacular remaking of classical material and the interplay of the sacred and the everyday—which, in Indian culture, are not stark opposites, but twinned and interactive poles on a sliding spectrum of possibilities. This remains true across the plurality of India's religions, including the Hindu, Buddhist, Christian, Islamic, Jain, Zoroastrian, Jewish, Sikh and other traditions.

The Sacred Everyday demonstrated this interrelationship across a variety of expressions, including calendar art, popular prints, shadow-puppet theatre, evocations of Mughal architecture, paracolonial painterly experiments at the cusp of Europe and Asia, masks, liturgical and ceremonial furniture, the recurrence of sacred geography and sacred geometry in religious art as well as modernist architecture, as well as the work of modernist and contemporary artists. This exhibition includes more than 200 objects from 13 individual, family, foundation and public collections, and has commissioned works by a number of artists.

The Sacred Everyday was installed at two venues, the Adil Shah Palace in Panjim and the Church of Santa Monica in Old Goa. At the church, the exhibition celebrated a first-ever collaboration between the Serendipity Arts Festival and a major Goa-based cultural institution, the Museum of Christian Art (MoCA). Inaugurated in 1994 at the Rachol Patriarchal Seminary, MoCA shifted, in 2001, to the Convent of Santa Monica, where it is now based. Since MoCA is currently under renovation, *The Sacred Everyday* offered an opportunity for some objects from its collection to be put on view, while inviting a new viewership to its precincts.

One of the key commitments of *The Sacred Everyday* is to erase the constraining and unproductive distinctions that segregate the "ancient," "mediaeval," "modern," "contemporary," "urban" and "folk" into separate compartments. These academic conveniences and connoisseurial prejudices have come to dictate our way of looking at cultural production and cultural producers, in ways that are profoundly damaging both to aesthetic experience and political engagement.

Dispensing with these categories, we can open our eyes and all our senses to the articulation of numerous local cultural realities. We encounter the unique practices that they have generated and nurtured—whether the transgressive popular iconographies of Kalighat and the chromolithographic "art studios" of nineteenth century Calcutta, with their cheeky reinterpretations of Hindu mythology; or the luminous sanctity of the Indo-Lusitanian Catholic sacred art of Goa, which is not reducible to any European or Indian "originals" but marks a particular and distinctive form of religious imagination; or the household or cottage-industry embellishment of Raja Ravi Varma's mythological chromolithographs with lace and other decorative details. Translation, transmutation and transfiguration are all vibrantly at work in these historical situations.

In the same spirit, to offer other examples, we dwell here on the wooden Gomira ancestor masks of Kushmundi in northern West Bengal, the Christological portraiture of A P da Cruz, the Expressionist handling of the Christ narrative by Vishwanath Nageshkar and the emphatically Indianised Christian iconography of Angelo da Fonseca; the neo-Tantric meditative paintings of the modernist Ghulam Rasool Santosh, the Jain mandala cosmology and the invocation of various paradigms of sacred architecture in the stellar oeuvre of Charles Correa; the persistence of the Kumari ceremonial in the work of Vidya Kamat, the celestial absorptions of Youdhishtir Maharjan, the evocation of existential residues and percussive fecundity by Smriti Dixit, and the preoccupation of Priya Pereira with gestures of prayer and remembrance. We address the work of South Indian artists active at the cusp of late-Mughal, Tanjore and European art and Eastern Indian artists at the cusp of Dutch art and Hindu mythology in what I have elsewhere described as the "Indo-Euro-Persianate ecumene" that was South Asia between the seventeenth and nineteenth centuries. Germane to our visual investigation and delight, also, are the extraordinary cultural and political dynamics played out in twentieth and twenty-first century South Asian calendar art. Observe as the Kamadhenu, the wish-fulfilling cow of Hindu lore, appears in the accoutrements of a Buraq from Islamic folklore, with wings and a peacock-feather tail. Observe as Ravi Varma's opulently costumed Lakshmi finds adjacency with a Kalighat-styled Lakshmi surrounded by the technological imagery of the Green Revolution.

We delight in the *Issa-nama* (2018)—a series of paintings rendered by Manish Soni in the manner of the Mughal imperial ateliers, the Rajput, Pahari and Safavid schools and illustrating episodes from the Life of Jesus. Looking at these paintings, I am reminded that the first-ever biography of Jesus to be published anywhere in the world was not written in a traditional Biblical language or for European readers — it was the *Mir'at al-Quds* or Mirror of Holiness, written in Persian by Jerome Xavier SJ, the grand-nephew of St Francis Xavier, for the Mughal emperor Akbar, and published in Agra, in 1602 AD.

The interrelationship between sacred and everyday that I map in this exhibition is partially based on the model of the margi and the desi as developed by the questor Ananda K. Coomaraswamy. Margi refers to the classical, elite, relatively abstract, pan-Indian cultural and religious apparatus, sometimes described as the Great Tradition (from marga, the pathway or route taken by the mriga, the black antelope). Desi refers to the robust, often though not necessarily subaltern, local and vernacular traditions of worship, storytelling, craft and poeisis, sometimes described as the Little Traditions (from desa, the region, the organic locality).

Typically, the Great Tradition conducts its business in Sanskrit; the Little Traditions prefer the local languages. The model can be extended, by parallel and analogy, beyond the Hindu-Buddhist universe with which it is associated. In a Christian setting, for instance, Jesuit theological speculation, with its accent on intellectual culture, coexists with the emotionally polychromatic Mariolatry of Vailankanni. In an Islamic context, likewise, the austere doctrinaire approach of the Tablighi or Wahhabi coexists with the sensuous and affective forms of worship associated with the Sufi dargah and ziarat.

This active interplay between margi and desi—a dialogue between the One and the Many—has been characterised, in various measures, by synchrony, opposition and the dramatic reshaping of icon and narrative. The One does not always prevail. It is more often absorbed within the elaborations of the Many. In my view, this interplay is often incarnated in the sthalapurana, the place legend—which, even as it absorbs the abstractions of the margi, is resolutely and even intransigently committed to the specificities of the desi. This exhibition invites its viewers to savour a variety of such sthala-puranas, place legends that inform—and form—our polyglot, unpredictable, paradoxical, porous and mercurial South Asian modernity.

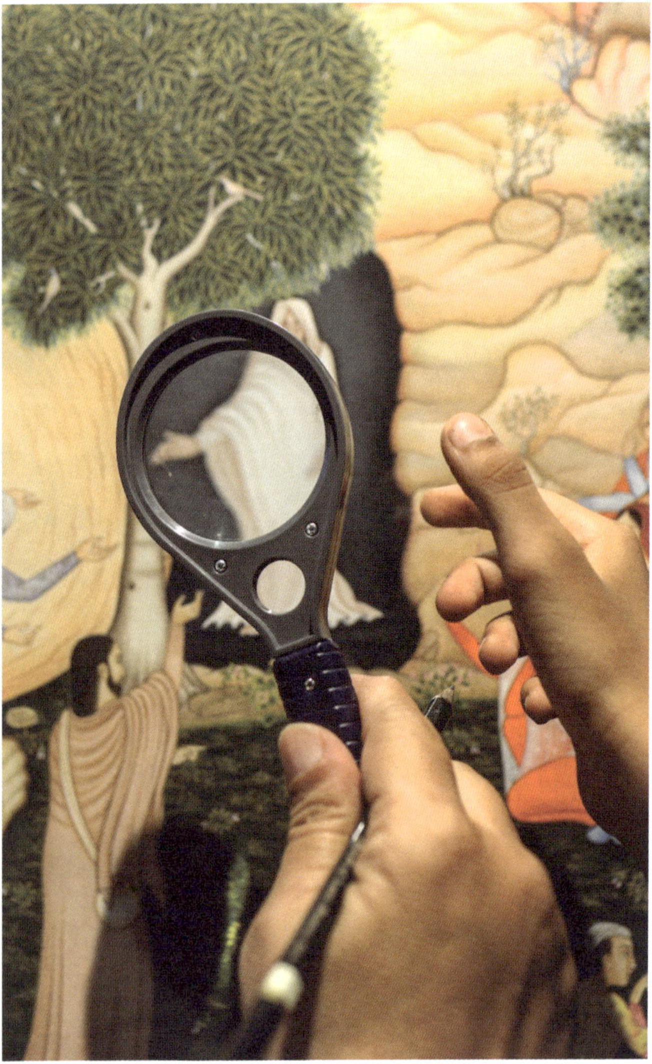

Detail of *Issanama* (2017-2018); Manish Soni; Series of 12; Opaque watercolour and natural pigments on hand-made paper; From the Sarmaya Arts Foundation, Mumbai

Lines of Flight: Confronting Syncretic Sacred Cultures

SENJUTI MUKHERJEE

> "The greatest rivers bear the most misleading names. The canon of geography dictates that the source furthest away from the mouth is the river's point of origin, and the entire watercourse takes on a single name. But no great river would reach the ocean without being fed by tributaries: the brooks, streams, rivulets that join its flow, often bringing with them more water, alluvium, minerals, or fish than the source stream. By the time the great river has reached the ocean, the source is no more than a faint memory; the flow has been defined by a series of confluences along the way. But the river's official name conceals the truth of its composition; while the nametag passes into legend and lexicon, the ancestry of confluences become invisible. To understand the true identity of the river, we would have to pinpoint the occasions of confluence, examine the dynamics of addition and innovation played out at the merging of the waters."
>
> - Ranjit Hoskote and Ilija Trojanow, *Confluences: Forgotten Histories from East and West*[1]

Ranjit Hoskote, in *Confluences*, a book he co-authored with Bulgarian-German author Ilija Trojanow, compares spuriously reconstructed history, synchronised to concepts of homogeneity and "pure" origin, to the way the tributaries, that build the identity of the great river, find no mention in seemingly singular nomenclature traditions. His exhibition *The Sacred Everyday* (2018) promises to traverse the "festive, playful, bottom-up impulses of improvisation" found in

India's pluralistic religious history. Bharatiya Janata Party, the Hindu fundamentalist and right-wing political party presently in power, along with their ideological ally Rashtriya Swayamsevak Sangh, are stuck in a paradox filled with fantasies about an "uncontaminated" Hindu nation in India, while endorsing open hostility and violence against minorities and minority traditions. This ongoing peddling of a shallow homogenous narrative definitively dissolves within the exhibition space as it attempts to embrace "the risk of difference" mentioned in the exhibition subtitle. The wall-text tries to speak lucidly to its audience, and Hoskote's disclaimer seems earnest: "This is not high culture. This is not academic theorising. This is the extraordinary character of the ordinary experience of a multi-layered, multi-dimensional, constantly self-transfiguring culture. This is the reality to which *The Sacred Everyday* bears witness."

With this exhibition, Hoskote identifies points of confluence and conflict within cultures through a rhythmically laid-out inquiry into iconography, ritual and mythic narrative. Confluence, as a concept that tries to illustrate cultural syncretism, is coined by Hoskote and Trojanow, and explored through the running metaphor of the river. The book insists: "When culture is alive, it alters itself through inspirations from the near and far, it changes its course. Culture is the eternal shape-shifter. Only by interacting with the Other, can culture keep itself alive. Thus, the greatest civilisations were built on confluence."[2]

The exhibition gives way to a metrical investigation of multiple co-ordinates concerning the sacred and the everyday divided along temporal lines: ancient, mediaeval, modern, contemporary; and cultural and aesthetic hierarchy: urban and folk. The reflection and unlearning of rigid classifications are facilitated by Coomaraswamy's approach to the Sanskritic aesthetic theory of *marga* (the classical, mainstream, pan-Indian aesthetic imagination) and *desi* (the regional or local vernacular traditions).

The Sacred Everyday seeks to unearth such confluences buried under myths of singularity: calling out falsified memories and contesting convenient amnesia—that obscures marginal histories and traditions—through a visual narrative. Unlike in experimental psychology, where amnesia is associated with repressed memory or violent unconsciousness; in Brahminical texts, it is considered the central attribute of human consciousness, while memory is a power independent of intellect. In his work investigating cultural amnesia of a post-colonial nation, G N Devy, a theorist, cultural activist and founder of the Adivasi Academy, refers to Coomaraswamy's re-interpretations of these Brahminical notions. Coomaraswamy re-defined memory as "a kind of latent knowledge" and amnesia as "a condition of the human mind," thereby, reformulating memory as the omniscient self and amnesia as its contingent ego.[3] Hoskote seemingly calls on a repressed memory of an anxious nation through the curation of this exhibition.

The Sacred Everyday is devoted to an exploration of trans-culturalism and pluralism, ideas that are central to Hoskote's other literary and curatorial work. Here, he builds on his meditations from previous exhibitions he curated for Serendipity Arts Festival in Panjim, Goa. *Terra Cognita?* (2016) celebrated the arrival of the printing press in Goa, the first region in Asia to have received the technology. The exhibition put together an evocative amalgam of printmaking from diverse times and places. *Anti-Memoirs* (2017) developed the idea of interaction between locus, language and landscape. He combined sculpture, painting, mass-published illustration, photo-installation, printmaking, archaeological documentation and stereoscopic entertainment to demonstrate shifts across time within the three interactive co-ordinates. In this exhibition, the curator's preoccupation with subverting established modes of representation made him concentrate on dissolving geographical and sequential barriers. In a phone conversation with me, the curator noted how this commitment to unlearning classifications is central to his curatorial process.

When asked if discarding the myopic yet neatly organised classifications of art and cultural traditions poses any inconvenience in the installation and layout planning process, Hoskote responded by highlighting that his fundamental interests are poetry, music and architecture, and these influence his approach to viewership. Drawing from poetic metre, his curatorial intent is to lay out a mixture of dense, intense, flamboyant spaces and muted, subdued spaces. A complex system of lines of flight and soft thresholds make up the rhythmic metre of the exhibition. "Lines of flight," a concept coined by Deleuze and Guattari, reveal that bolts of suppressed energy sometimes escape through the cracks in an authoritarian system and shoot off—lighting their passage as they go. In this light, new spaces are unveiled, beyond the limits of what is being represented by the systems of control.[4] He refers to the spaces he creates within the exhibition as "zones of intensity" tied together by contact, overlap and confluence.

One of the key protagonists of the exhibition was its venue, the Adil Shah Palace in Goa. The history of this space foregrounds the central themes of the exhibition in many ways. The place pre-dates its colonial architectural identity: originally the summer palace and fortress of Bijapur's Yusuf Adil Shah, the palace was invaded and taken over by Portuguese troops led by Afonso de Albuquerque in 1510. Around 1759, the Palace of Bijapur became the Idalcaon Palace, the Viceroy's official residency. The demolitions and renovations of this period changed the building's façade, bringing it closer to its appearance today. The second batch of transformation occurred during Goa's liberation from the Portuguese in 1961: the building embraced its new identity as home to Goan State Legislature and came to be known as the Secretariat. Since then, the Secretariat has moved across the blue expanse of the Mandovi River, making space for administrative offices of the new government. Currently, the space has been partially re-purposed to host arts and culture events; Serendipity Foundation renovated the building during their 2016 festival. The building continues to be surrounded by emblems representing various temporal layers of the city surface: visible from the palace are the Mhamai Kamath House, home to the Empire's financiers; a statue of Abbe Faria, an eighteenth-century transcultural figure famous for yoga and hypnotism; and a statue of Dayanand Bandodkar, the first elected chief minister of liberated Goa.

THE SACRED INTERIOR

The exhibition begins by conjuring up the interior spaces of individual homes where popular and calendar prints originally belong. The first "zone" comprises the popular as well as the domestic. A dramatic collision of images sourced from Swaraj Art Archive and the Jyotindra & Jutta Jain Collection is presented in this room. The extensive wall-text explains the growth of new popular imagery in nineteenth-century India, fostered by the emergence of printmaking techniques, photography and theatre. Here, viewers notice tempera paintings on board, the "original" artworks that led to calendar prints—the latter being the epitome, in some sense, of mass-produced objects disregarded in the world of arts due to an inherent lack of "aura," a concept coined by Walter Benjamin. Introduced in the essay "The Work of Art in the Age of Mechanical Reproduction," aura is defined as an original artwork's unique existence in time and space as well as its aesthetic authority. Does Hoskote's decision to exhibit the original work, lead to a retrieval of the missing aura of calendar arts in our understanding, or did it intend to dispute the graveness of the aura's significance?

I looked at the wall where the calendar prints hang in two different ways. Primarily, as individual images: religious, mythic, epic and familial icons of piety appear against romanticised landscapes in them, most of which date back to the 1940s and '50s. These popular prints, belonging to geographically diverse sources, borrowed their aesthetic from Indian miniature traditions to the art of Shantiniketan and Bombay School of Art. These narrate the pluralistic atmosphere of religious landscapes. The emblematic image of an aristocratic-looking goddess Lakshmi by Raja Ravi Varma School is closely accompanied by C Kondiah Raju's portrayal of Hindu deities in middle-class southern Indian clothing and ornamentation.

I also viewed the whole wall as one composite image, which reminded me of another, similar image: that of the interiors of homes in Bhatisuda village, in Christopher Pinney's book *The Photos of Gods*.

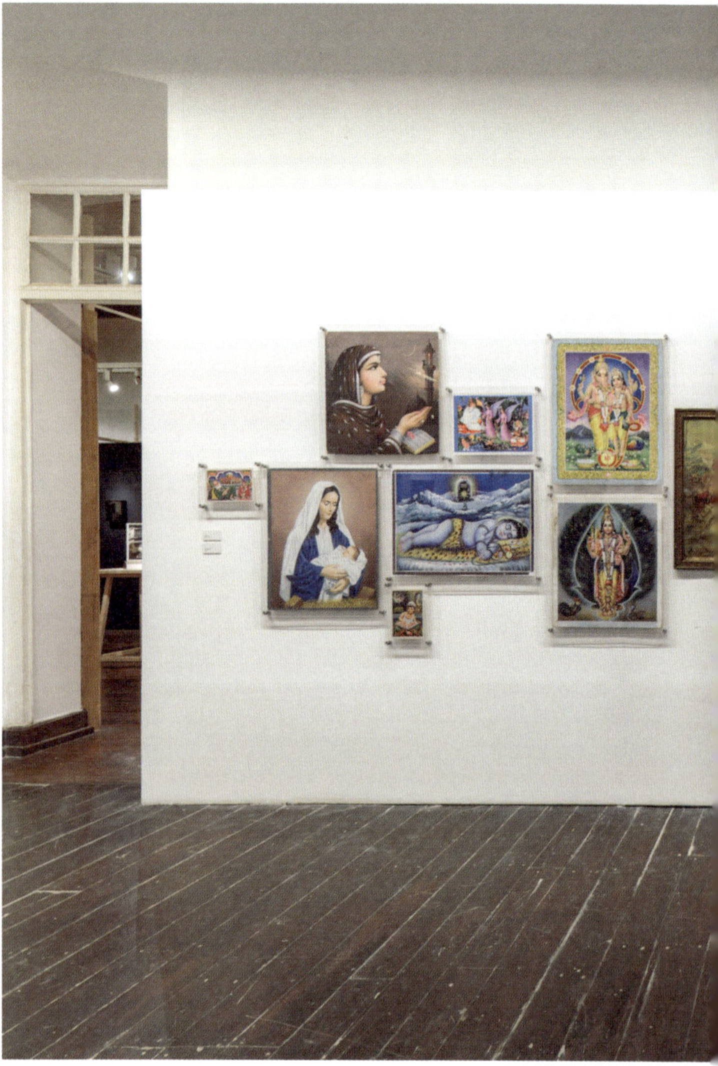

Installation view of Popular prints; Tempera on board; From the Swaraj Art Archive, Noida and Popular Islamic prints (c. 1990); Offset prints; Courtesy Jyotindra & Jutta Jain

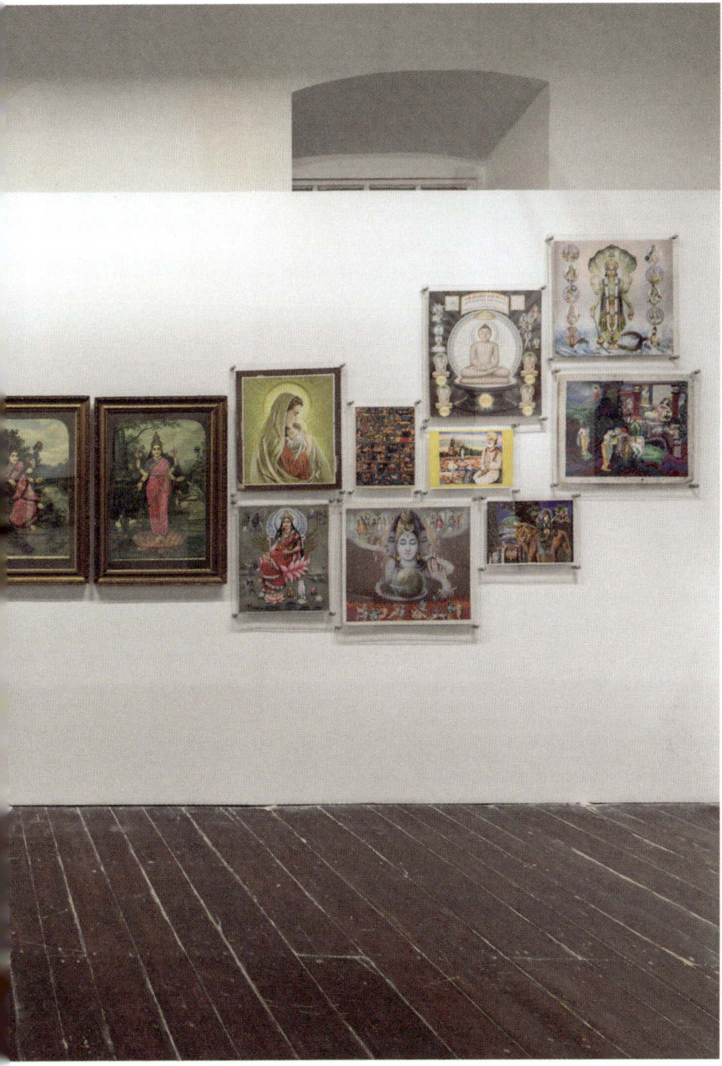

Pinney marvels at the capacity of such images to rework patterns of worship. Formal aesthetic criteria are of little to no importance in his evaluation of these images; instead, it is the ability of the object to intervene in the world which makes it compelling: "As Pannalal performs this puja, appealing for a protective plenitude in the face of harsh uncertainties, he murmurs to himself, waves his incense sticks, rings a small bell and crumbles whatever marigolds might be lying on the puja shelf in front of his images. As he does this his eyes maintain an intense visual intimacy with the gods and his body describes a gentle swaying, yearning, movement as though caught in the force-field around the image."[5]

Recounting this anecdote from Pinney's book in an exhibition laid out in the museum-style and trying to imagine a force-field possible only within interior and personal spaces is a fitting moment to return to the title of the exhibition—*The Sacred Everyday*. The title seemed to have suddenly come to life as one recalls consumers seeking to make religious experience as malleable, tangible and accessible as possible, particularly those who are deemed unworthy of the religious sanctoriums. In this regard, Pinney refers to Jean-François Lyotard while trying to comprehend sacred images in this intimate interior space: "For Lyotard, the figural is 'relatively free of the demands of meaning', indeed it is not the arena for the production of meaning but a space where 'intensities are felt'."[6]

At a later point in my viewing of the exhibition, in a related but different zone of intensity, Smriti Dixit's work *Yatra* (2018) evoked a sense of the intimate interior space. This installation travels from the intimate and the individual to the collective in its inquiry into different layers of memory through an array of shelves with personal, domestic objects, such as utensils of plastic, glass, stainless steel, aluminum and brass, which belong to the kitchen, eating place, and the prayer room. Near these vessels, on another shelf, seamlessly appear a grandfather's inherited Bhagawat Gita and a partly written, partly scribed album with intimate images representing chroniclers of a different register of memory. A sawn part of a tree-trunk found in the

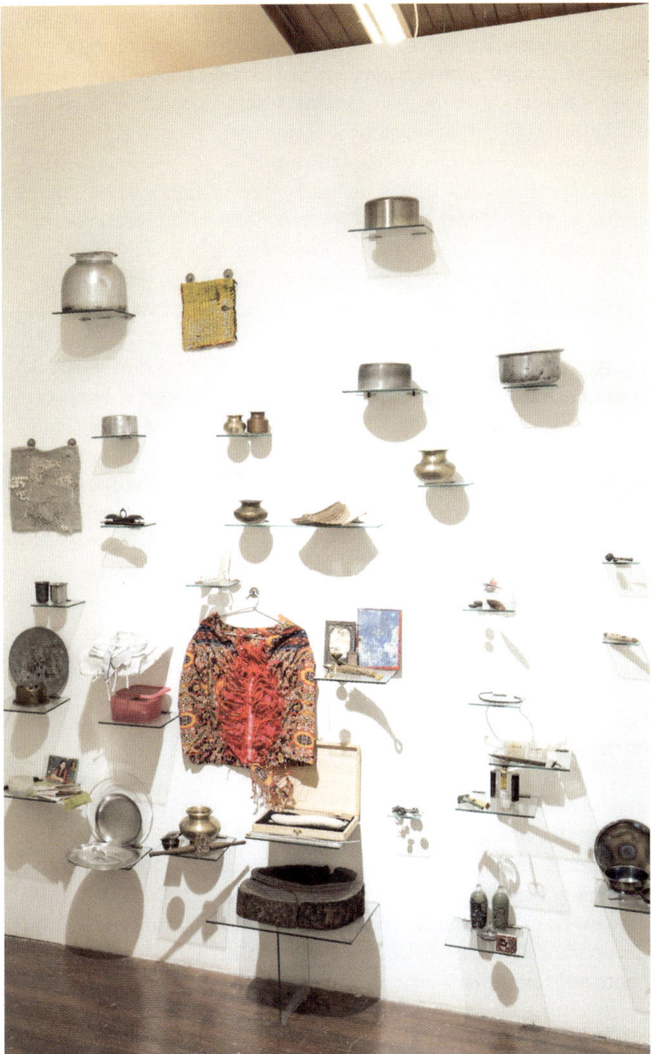

Yatra (2018); Smriti Dixit; Aluminium, brass, cloth, cotton, glass, paper, plastic, seeds, silver, steel, synthetic fabric and wood; Courtesy Art Musings, Mumbai

street is placed under an old garment hanging from the wall, holding out against obsolescence. Part of the wall-text accompanying the installation reads: "Yatra suggests both a domestic arrangement and a laboratory in which the residues of a life, markers of biographical passage, may be considered and dwelled upon."

While I was looking at Dixit's reconstruction of a laboratory of the interior, A K Ramanujan's translations of *Cankam* (*Sangam*) poetry came to mind. Classical Cankam (Sangam) poetry is divided into two main components: *Akam* or love poetry and *Puram* or war poetry. These two categories are analogous with marga and desi as both are considered spatial and sociocultural inventions. Akam relates to the interior space—the space of the heart, mind, household, the self and kin, and is explored through love poems. Puram is poetry about war, a public poetry of sorts, based around real people and places. The somewhat unexplored but incredibly sublime thing about Akam, the poetry of the inner world, is that it's organised on the basis of geographical landscapes such as forests, mountains, pastoral regions and the sea-shore, presided over, respectively, by the deities *Mayon* (*Visnu*), *Murukan*, *Ventan* (*Indra*) and *Varuna*. Where is the interior in such an instance, if according to Cankam (Sangam) literature natural landscapes belong to the interior domain presided over by deities? When the sacred belongs to the interior landscape, it's infused with immense potential for spontaneity and myriad forms, as the domestic space becomes synonymous with the little traditions—unscripted, oral and interactive.

The evoked space of the contemporary art installation somewhat matches the imagined space where the popular prints belong—the home, the interior, although separate in time, sentiment and aesthetic sensibility. Various layers of memory are found sitting on suspended shelves, ranging from kitchen vessels to a found part of a tree-trunk, old textile and garment, a grandfather's inherited copy of the Gita, a photo and text album—all withstanding amnesia and obsolescence.

Is there then a composite and interactive network of little traditions in all domestic spaces, if little traditions can be understood as one without a written scripture? Do photo albums, garments, and metallic vessels maintain the sacred decree of the domestic fold? Does the interior space nurture people and communities by playing out their improvised, fascinating and abundant religious and social roles?

ARCHITECTURE AS MODEL FOR THE COSMOS

The allure of the landscape as interior space next enters a zone of direct reflection on built spaces, with photographs of three buildings by Charles Correa: Jaipur Kala Kendra in Jaipur (1986-1992), the Inter University Centre of Astronomy and Astrophysics in Pune (1988-1992) and the Salvacaco Church in Bombay (1974-1977). These images of stark and magnificent sandstone and concrete poetry are represented at the centre of this zone and surrounded by Mughal Architecture Drawings as well as Yudhishthir Mahajan's commissioned works. Correa's work contemplates the notions of Sacred Geometry consisting of diagrams and symbols from religious traditions and Sacred Geography consisting of revered mountains, forests, confluence of rivers.

Correa was greatly invested in noticing and animating the remnants of the Sacred in our modern urban world. He wrote about how religion, philosophy and the arts were interactive notions, and they belonged in, what he called the non-manifest world. This world, that can be recognised through religious traditions, philosophy and the arts, is a platform for sacred gestures and iconographies, in an otherwise commercial landscape that's made to appear increasingly homogenous on the surface.

Two intriguing projects are juxtaposed against each other on one side of the false wall here—Salvacao church in Mumbai and IUCAA in Pune—Correa's own reflections on the intimacy between the sacred and the scientific. Originally built in Baroque style in 1596 by the Portuguese, the Salvacao church was rebuilt and renovated several times before Correa revamped it between 1974 and 1977. Through this project he introspects on the possibilities Church typology could have had if historical narrative played out differently: if, instead of locating its development in Europe, Christianity got its iconographies from Asia, its birth-continent. The steeples, choir loft, ascending roof and ornate façade disappeared one after the other during the years he worked on the building, to be replaced by a stark conical concrete composition of modern times. Wind and light are his elementary concerns and concrete his medium of expression. The poetry is made possible by the poet's meditation on what he calls the *invisibilia* of everyday life, or the sacred everyday. In his essay "The Public, the Private, and the Sacred," he maps the natural progression from stone to plant to animal to humans, from material to sacred:

"For everything essential in our fellow human beings—their thoughts, emotions, aspirations, fantasies—are invisible to us. These invisibilia are of infinitely greater power and significance than the visibilia of everyday life."[7]

Nature and climate foreground the architect's meditations on the built form. Images of the Salvacao church in the exhibition reveal the skylight letting in light through the concrete shell roof, as if built with the purpose of letting in and highlighting the divinity ensconced in light.

Charles Correa's writings reveal his preoccupation with "open to the sky" spaces. He reflects on how the word *aakash* connotes a different range of things than the word "sky" does. In an attempt to further explain this ineffable range an individual is conditioned to access through these spaces, he draws a comparison between the symbol of education in North America and Asia. While the former is represented by the little red schoolhouse, the latter is a wide landscape with the teacher sitting under a tree.[8] Correa also commissioned M F Hussain, a modernist painter to draw the mural on this skylight—uniting religions and expressing the sacred through climate, concrete and modernism.

Reference images of this building are juxtaposed with that of the Inter

University Centre for Astronomy and Astrophysics in Pune. Here, Correa re-interprets landscape as a reproduction of the cosmos, celebrating interactive diagrams of ancient mysticisms and modern physics, mandalas and non-linear mathematics. This experiment is integral to the architect's philosophy, in which he marvels at the scientific in the sacred, the pluralism within knowledge forms. Although *Vastu Purush Mandalas* form the basis of his modernist architecture, such mandalas are not intended to be plans for building making; their original intention is to represent an energy field. The centre of the mandala signifies a concept related to astrophysics: both *shunya* (the absolute void) and *bindu* (the world seed and source of all energy) simultaneously. The theory of general relativity states that energy consumes itself, and all mass goes down the vortex of energy in the centre of the black hole, where no light is reflected, and no escape can be planned. This abstraction is meticulously translated into architectural patterns in the Black Hole Courtyard of the campus at IUCAA. The paths inside the campus are lined with basalt walls topped with black granite, an architectural metaphor for the formless and dark outer space, dividing the campus into three courtyards. The *kund* or the courtyard hosts three spectacular statues of scientists, remindful of those of gods. Throughout the courtyards, landscape elements are arranged to symbolise different cosmic images from physics and sacred geometry. These vary from the Sierpinski fractal—a decorative element that was present in the arts centuries before the Polish mathematician Sierpinski invented the fixed set of the equilateral triangle that can be subdivided recursively to smaller equilateral triangles—to the preservation of two neighbouring trees in the complex to form the Roche Lobes, a binary system or diagram of an orbiting planet's gravitationality to a star.

On the backside of this wall are images of Correa's Jaipur Kala Kendra, or the JKK, a project he took up in 1986. He was inspired by Sawai Jai Singh II, the seventeenth-century scholar, mathematician, astronomer, and king, whose plan of Jaipur was heavily influenced by the *Shilpa Shastra* and the tenets of the Vastu Purush Mandala. The city's layout was guided by the nine squares or houses of the Mandala

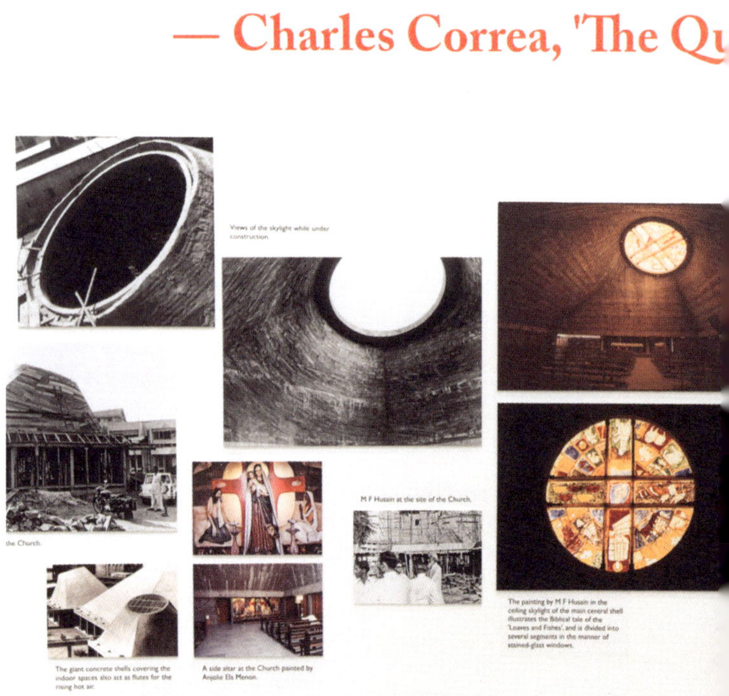

Architectural projects of Charles Correa; Salvacao Church, Bombay (1974-1977); Courtesy Charles Correa Foundation, Goa

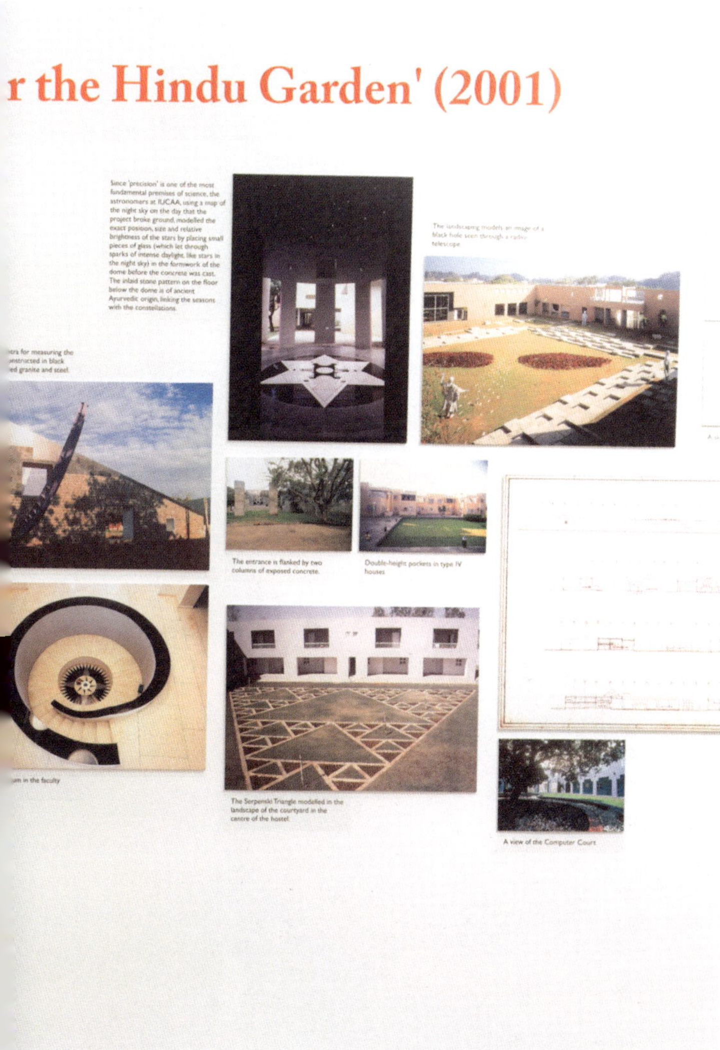

Architectural projects of Charles Correa; IUCAA, Pune (1988-1992);
Courtesy Charles Correa Foundation, Goa

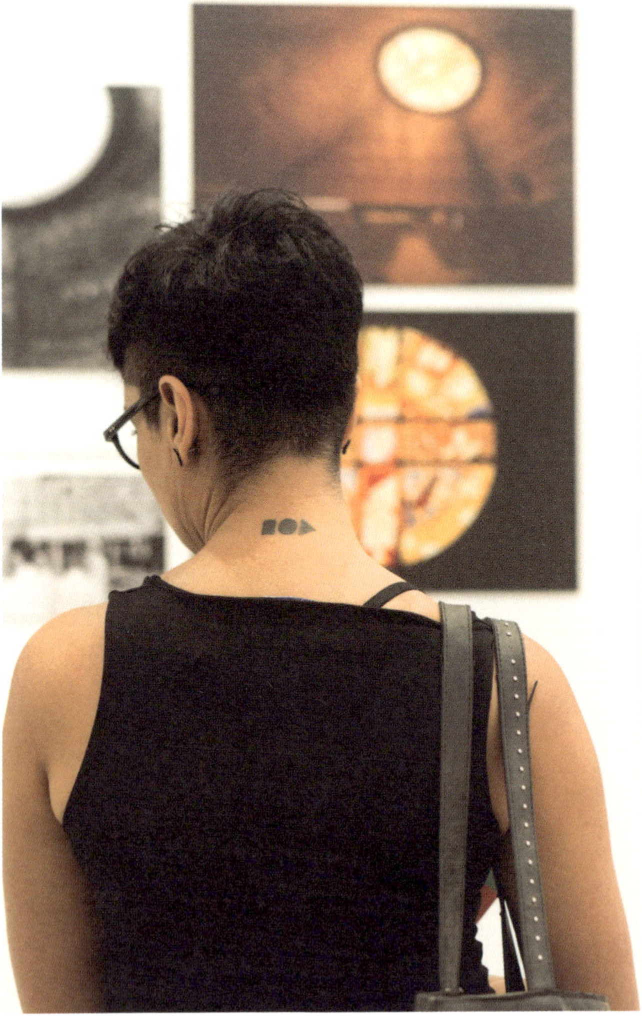

Installation view of architectural projects of Charles Correa

that represent the nine planets. Correa's planning for the JKK directly invoked this *Navagraha* (nine planets) model. These images from Correa's works are surrounded by many other compelling images in deliberate dialogues with each other. These include sacred religious images such as a Jain Mandala, a Fakir's Kabah, a Sufi shrine, a Jyotirlinga map, as well as nine nineteenth-century water-colours of Mughal architecture in Agra, including Akbar's tomb in Sikandra and the Fatehpur Sikri: both of which are exemplary instances of Mughal architectural experimentations. Fatehpur Sikri is unlike most other Islamic complexes, which usually boast of axial plans with buildings centrally located in Char-Bagh garden spaces. A sequentially organised complex of interlinking and enclosed open-spaces and courtyards, Sikri turns away from the hierarchical spatial orders of Islamic architecture and planning. Similarly, Akbar's tomb in Sikandra is a liberal assemblage of disparate architectural motifs and incorporates a large variety of Hindu architectural elements. Hoskote, in this section, continues to unravel narratives of syncretism and pluralism by setting up dialogues between diverse artistic practices.

MARGA AND DESI - THE HIGHWAY AND THE PLACE

Marga in Sanskrit means "the way" or "the high road," and Desi means "the place," "the locale" or "the country road," therefore, both words literally denote two different kinds of spaces as aesthetic and cultural hierarchies. The first signifies the classical, mainstream, supra-regional "great traditions," and the latter signifies the local, vernacular, inaccurately termed "little traditions." India's critical writing history has witnessed plenty of engagement with these terms in the fields of performing arts, literary forms, and modern sociology.

Kapila Vatsyayan writes about AK Coomaraswamy's re-interpretation of these Sanskritic aesthetic categories: "Coomaraswamy... clearly sees the logic of the marga as the dug path, a highway which is constantly on the move but in a particular direction with a specific purpose. It may perhaps be more appropriate to see what

Coomaraswamy calls desi or a 'by-way'... as the circumscribing or limiting of eternal universal paths into the mannerisms or styles of a region or a given time situation. Indeed, from this point of view the two terms appear to connote not levels of society but only universalisation and specificity. This is certainly not what the terms 'classical' and 'folk' in common parlance denote... The cognisance of the possibility of the margi becoming the desi at any given moment is inherent in the very nature of their relationship."[9]

Vatsyayan herself has engaged and investigated these hallowed categories in her critical writing and has pointed out that the Sanskrit root of marga is *mrg*, which means chasing or hunting the hidden light down the highway. Desi, on the other hand, derives from *dis*, meaning region, quarter and local. It's only in modern sociology that marga and desi have come to denote town/city or village respectively. But if these aesthetic terms are understood and applied through their re-interpretations by Coomaraswamy and Vatsyayan, the concepts become replaceable, relatable and equivalent. The rejection of imported western theoretical apparatuses made a lot of Indian intellectuals and critics turn to Sanskritic aesthetic devices like the marga-desi in the 1980s. It is important to note here that there was debate and skepticism regarding this critical turn as well. Ayappa Paniker and the American critic John Oliver Perry were known to have warned critics from falling into the homogenising trap of "Indianness" in Sanskrit poetics without re-purposing them.

Stone busts/sculptures of *Gram Devatas, Devis*, and *Malhara* sourced from Goa State Museum near the images of Charles Correa's works are at the heart of a compelling conversation that takes place between the categories of marga-desi. Gram Devata is the Sanskrit name for the deity that presides over a village, falling under the faulty category of desi traditions. Different regions have differing deities, the gram devata figure in Goa originated from the prevalent worship of *yakshas* and *kshetrapalas*, guardians of the interior landscape like in Akam poetry: the home, fields, water sources and forests. Similarly, the worship of the devis is associated with the cult of *Saptamatrikas*,

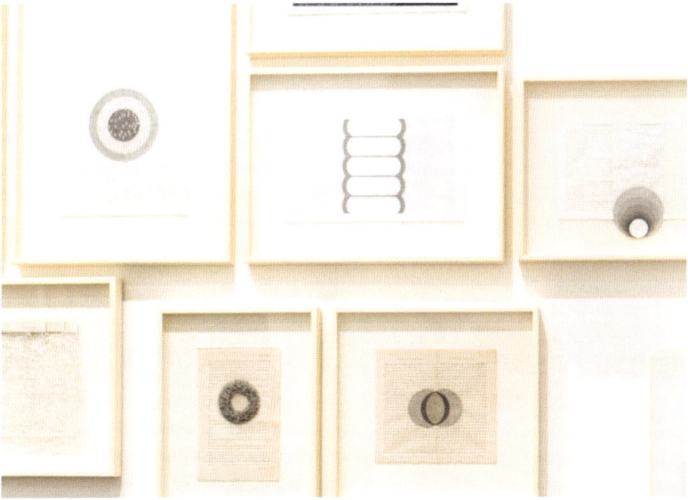

Installation view of works by Youdhisthir Maharjan; Acrylic, graphite, coloured pencil, and hand-cut text collage on deacidified, reclaimed book pages; 2018; Courtesy Blurprint12, New Delhi

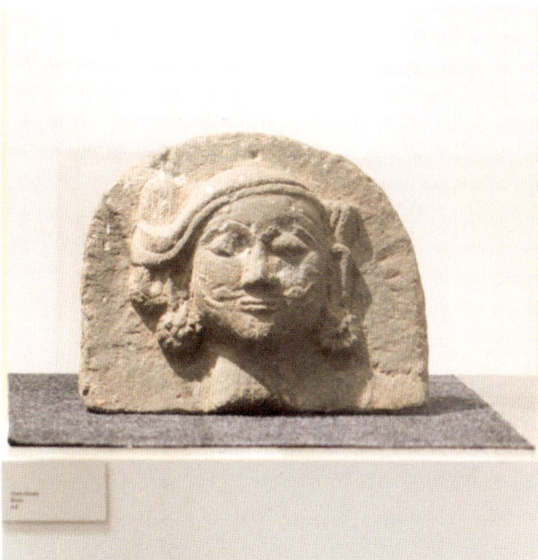

Gram Devata, n.d.; Stone; From the Goa State Museum

paramount goddesses of mainstream Hindusim. The wall-text highlights how these cults have overlapped in the past. The third kind of guardian figure that's seen here is a Malhara, popularly known as a *Khandoba*. The wall-text reminds the viewer that this desi deity of the little traditions found its place within the marga or pan-Indian "great tradition" of Shaivism as Martand Bhairava.

Tantra-inspired paintings by GR Santosh, a celebrated painter of modern Indian art, neighbour these devis and devatas. Unlike the stone busts, Santosh's paintings have come to be commercially successful: habitually gracing big galleries and, museums, and being treasured objects of the art market and auction sales. These, in turn, rhythmically lead to the wooden *Gomira* masks from the traditional Gomira dance from Kushmandi Village, in North Dinajpur district, in West Bengal. The word Gomira finds its desi roots in the local Shakti deity *Gram Chandi*. Hoskote's exhibition layout cuts across the slippery categories of marga and desi by presenting and considering one in the close presence of the other. In the same space, he leads a deliberate conversation between Kalighat Pats and what he terms as "Tourism Tantra." The latter comprises kitschy contemporary paintings meant for tourist consumption, made by anonymous Rajasthani artists. By placing them next to the musealised popular prints like Kalighat Pat, he probes whether, in its time, Kalighat Pat (born not of any art school or movement but a crowded neighbourhood market of a pilgrimage centre) was viewed in the same way as popular prints from Rajasthan today.

In a cleverly designed double-sided gallery, colourful puppets from Andhra Pradesh are displayed in the first and the last rooms of the exhibition. *Tholubommalata*, literally translates as the dance of the leather puppets, is a form of shadow puppetry, a living tradition that traverses many genres of fantasy-making. A predecessor to cinema, the narration is constructed through shadows of moving puppets falling on temporary screens while wandering entertainers narrate tales and sing ballads. Of all forms of shadow puppetry, Tholubommalata came closest to cinematic fantasies as it

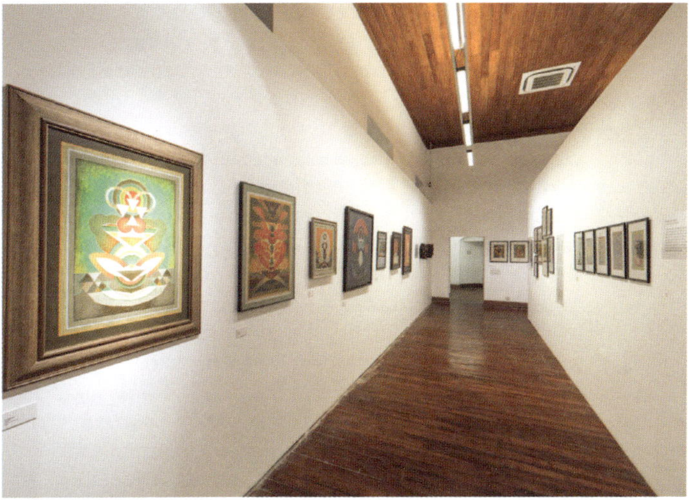

Untitled (1989); G R Santosh;
Acrylic on canvas; From the Swaraj Art Archive, Noida

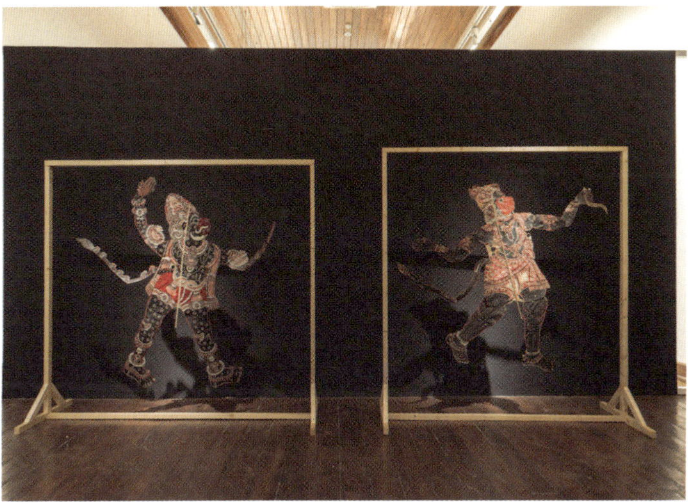

Left: *Tholubommalata puppet of Hanuman* (2015-16); S. Chidambara Rao; Perforated and dyed leather; From the Sarmaya Arts Foundation, Mumbai
Right: *Tholubommalata puppet of Hanuman* n.d.; Perforated and dyed leather; From the Swaraj Art Archive, Noida

constructed a Technicolour illusion using a special kind of puppet. Goat, buffalo and deer skin is beaten to translucency and coloured with vegetable dyes to make the puppets, the translucent skin facilitating the colour of the puppets, to make colourful shadows on the screen. Performances often last all night, while the holes in the puppets allow light through and sparkle like stars as they move across the frames. With the arrival of traveling cinemas (a dying form today), Tholubommalata lost its unique place in the fantasy world of Hindu epic narratives and local folk traditions.

Hoskote undergoes an extensive process of un-categorising and dismantling visual and material culture through a non-hierarchical exhibition layout. He elucidates on his approach in a phone conversation with me: "These categories hold very little meaning. They could be useful academic terminology but it's dangerous to have them influence your way of perceiving art and art history. This is a positivist evolutionary way of documenting phases of development and coming up with end results where one is more advanced or primitive than the other. Working in the art world for three decades makes one privilege the modernist and the contemporary artworks over other forms, and the last few years my approach has been more trans-historical and attempt has been to present the categories to break them down, cutting at an angle across these hierarchies."

MANUFACTURING HOMOGENOUS SPACE

> "Space is political. Space is not a scientific object removed from ideology or politics; it has always been political and strategic."
>
> - Henri Lefebvre, *Reflections on the Politics of Space*[10]

Lefebvre, the spatial theorist, highlights how subjection, domination, exploitation, and power relations—both repressive and productive—are implicitly spatial. Foucault, in his exploration of spatial turns also attempts to examine power at the site it operates in. It is space, with its embodiment of historical sediments and cultural agency, where power is constituted, exercised and resisted.

In the last room of the exhibition, near the Tholubommalata puppets, the viewer encounters an image of *Mahishasura-Mardini* seated under Chinese-style clouds, floating in an image space that draws its aesthetic quality from commercial film posters, comic books and miniature paintings. Besides, this room hosts a dialogue within the space of literary texts, as well as questioning the canonical status of epics such as the *Mahabharata* or the *Maha-Ithihasa*, the *Ramayana* or the *Maha-Kavya*: Hanuman is the curious figure that traverses the space-time of history and across the epics, as he serves a cameo in *Mahabharata* as Bhima's older brother, both being sons of the wind god Vayu. Amid all of these is an image of *Ayappa*, the deity of the Sabarimalai temple and a figure whose significance is somewhat eclipsed today, with the temple mired in political controversy. In September 2018, the Supreme Court of India ruled that pilgrims including women of menstruating age will be allowed inside the temple, which formerly banned the same. This led to protests led by Hindutva organisations opposing the verdict.

Ayappa, the son of Shiva and Mohini, the female avatar of Vishnu, seems to find no mention in any of the classical major texts or the marga traditions. The performances of rituals and vows practised amongst the pilgrims closely resemble those endorsed in the Buddhist doctrine of *ahimsa*. Besides, there's been some consensus within scholarly circles that Ayappa could be a form of *Nilakantha Avalokiteswara* from the Buddhist Puranas.

Hoskote emphasises in a conversation with me, that the sacred complex of the Sabarimalai temple hosts a shrine of a Muslim Deity *Vavar*, as well as the Arthunkal church. This heterogeneous space might have been made possible by the deity's desi status, where the lack of a formal doctrine helps conjoint religious and social practices thrive more easily. Consequently, the identity of the deity is eclectic as is the location of the controversial temple, and the nature of the journey the pilgrims take through this space. The Brahminisation of this worship has picked up momentum in recent decades; the misogynistic rule against women entering the shrine was enforced only in 1950. Hindutva supporters have since attempted to erase the historical dimensions and features of spaces such as the Sabarimalai.

When I asked about his thoughts on the controversy and the decision to pick this work, Hoskote emphasises that, beneath the uproar and agitation lays the inaccurate Brahminical re-purposing of the inherently pluralistic space.

THE PORTABLE ALTAR AS A PORTAL TO THE HOLY HILL

A portable altar at the Adil Shah exhibition serves as a connecting point to the concurrent part of the exhibition housed in Santa Monica church. Sourced from the Museum of Christian Art in Old Goa, the altar displayed is a wooden box devoid of ornamentation or any painting on the exterior. Intended to be the centrepiece of the liturgical space of the church, the space of the box expands in meaning when opened, as it is occupied by sacred texts. The two brackets of the lid support lights instead of ordinary candlesticks. Another section unfolds to turn into an altar top that comes with a centrally placed altar stone, large enough for the celebration of the Eucharist. A drawer in the box holds various liturgical and other accoutrements making it a sacred free-standing structure.

Like the Adil Shah Palace, the Santa Monica church was restored in 2016. Architecturally a coming together of the Tuscan and Corinthian orders, this church sits delightfully on the Holy Hill in Old Goa. During a phone conversation, Hoskote reflected on the space of the Santa Monica Church as an exhibition venue. He emphasised the entirely different calibration that is a prerequisite to working in a sacred space. The thematic element that holds together this half of the show is the curator's inquiry into the Indianisation of Christian imagery. Hoskote told me in a phone conversation: "One has to think

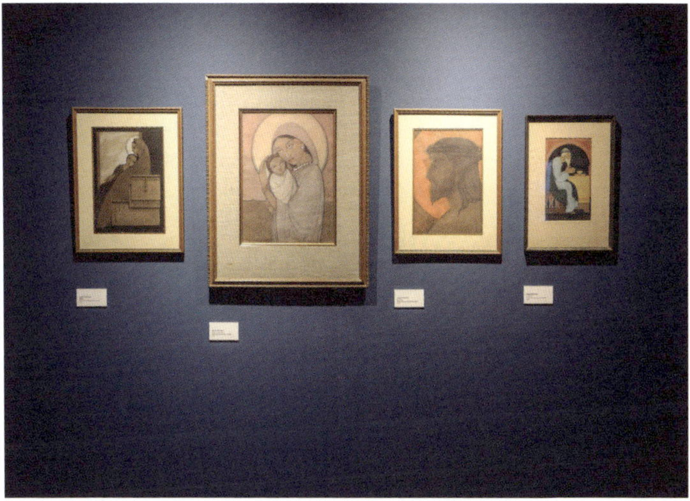

Installation view of paintings by Angelo da Fonseca; From Leonard and Naomi Menezes Collection, Goa

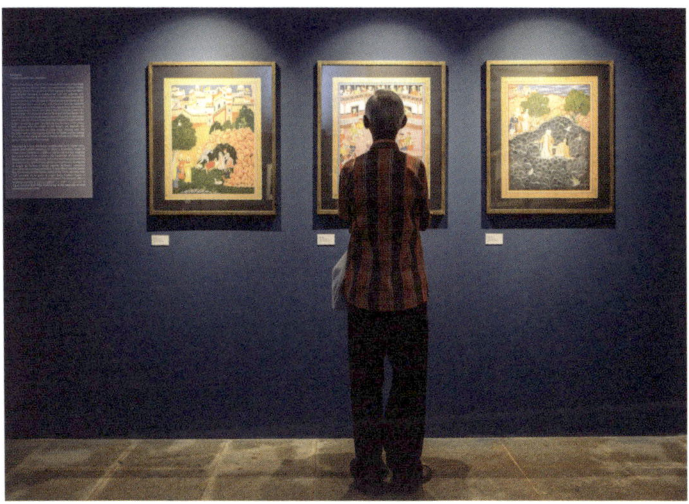

Installation view of *Issanama* (2017-2018); Manish Soni; Series of 12; Opaque watercolour and natural pigments on hand-made paper; From the Sarmaya Arts Foundation, Mumbai

through Christianity's non-colonial and para-colonial presence. For instance, I've been fascinated by the first biography of Jesus called *Mirat Ul Quds* that was written in Persian for Akbar."

Besides popular prints, sourced from the Swaraj Archive, showing Jesus entering Jerusalem and a Noah's Ark from Karachi, that draws its aesthetic inspiration from Hollywood film posters, there's a series of works by the controversial Goan painter Angelo da Fonseca at the Santa Monica.

During a stint at medical college, where Angelo da Fonseca was popular for his brilliant anatomical drawings, he realised that his passion lay in art. Unimpressed by the conformist Eurocentric training at J. J. School of Art, Fonseca travelled to Shantiniketan in West Bengal to learn from Abanindranath Tagore, an exponent of, what R. Sivakumar called, contextual modernism. The iconic printed picture or painting of a pale-skinned Madonna wearing a modest robe hanging in the brown-skinned Goan Catholic household found a new vocabulary in Fonseca's art. His paintings have delicate lines and earth-colours, while Virgin Mary is draped in Goan Kunbi sarees and placed in aesthetically local spaces, thereby re-inventing the iconographic vernacular. Goan art historian Savia Viegas writes: "The Roman Catholic Church took umbrage against his renderings of a brown skinned Madonna and various saints. Also, neither the colonial government nor common people were in any mood to re-clothe the Virgin Mother and the pantheon of saints in Indian garb."[11]

Goan religious cultures being historically segregated into the Hindus and Catholics with different sets of aesthetic and iconographic resources, Fonseca's paintings naturally seemed threatening to the Eurocentric Catholic religious identity. Through these Indian Christian paintings, the artist located the sacred or the divine in his spatio-cultural context, acknowledging and paying homage to the heterogeneous and composite postcolonial modern Indian identity. Criticism from the local church and priest made him shift to Pune. His paintings seem to have the intention of carrying out a two-fold desire of locating the religious within his cultural geography by imagining aesthetic features linked to the religion's Asiatic roots as well as locating the sacred in the everyday and domestic by often drawing the faces of the women in his household. Looking at Fonseca's ethereal works in the space of the church recalls his own deliberations about the nature of his art. Considering painting a spiritual dedication, Savia Viegas writes: "Fonseca rejected the salon in favour of smaller exhibitions in church halls and municipal buildings. He wanted god to be drawn from within the church precincts and to live in the community."[12]

Continuing his explorations along the same conceptual thread, but across artistic movements and expressions, Hoskote presents contemporary artist Priya Pereira's work *The Holy Rosary* (2004) in the same space. Pereira, a book artist, explores stories of folklore and tradition through her elegant works. Three of her works are laid out next to Dixit's Yatra in Adil Shah Palace: *The Wish Grill* (2003) is a work inspired by Akbar's prayer to Sheikh Salim Chishti for male heirs, while *Double-crossing a River* (2005) looks at how folktales were used to convert locals to Christianity in the early seventeenth century. Mirage probes the very existential dilemma of the seen and the unseen, and the likelihood of faith being an illusion. *The Holy Rosary* at the Santa Monica explores the author's personal story: in keeping with the concerns of this space, the work considers a Tamil daughter-in-law's desire to make an impression on her Catholic mother-in-law. The pages of the book illustrate beads of the rosary and mosaic patterns inform the viewer of the number of times the prayer is to be recited.

With this work, we return to our reflections on the improvised sacred space of the home, the interior, where filial longings sometimes affect sacred practices.

ARKHEION UNSETTLED

> "Let us not begin at the beginning, nor even at the archive. But rather at the word archive and with the archive of so familiar

> a word. Arkhe we recall, names at once the commencement and the commandment. This name apparently coordinates two principles in one: the principle according to nature or history, there where things commence—physical, historical, or ontological principle—but also the principle according to the law, there where men and gods command, there where authority and social order are exercised, in this place from which order is given—nomological principle."
> - Jacques Derrida, "Archive Fever: A Freudian Impression"[13]

This spatial exploration of the archive through etymological queries is what Derrida attempts to do in his complex text, "Archive Fever." The essay focusses primarily on the impact of electronic media on public and private spaces of humanity, as well as the connection between the archive and structures of human memory. The aspects that interest me are the spatial claims revealed by the etymological survey of the word. The Greek work "Arkhe" determines this space of the archive as one of commencement and commandment—historically binding the archival space to the government, power and law. The Greek origin of the word "Arkheion," Derrida explains initially referred to "a house, a domicile, an address of the superior magistrates, the archons, those who commanded." The essay established a close connection between the archival space and that of political power.

Various subversive and radical collections and archives are disseminating information unsparingly today. Besides, personal or family collections and archives are often drawn upon and mobilised for display by curators of external institutions and independent historians. Hoskote, in the exhibition, sets in motion vast portions from archives of varying expanse and compositions. The archives of Correa are drawn from an institution founded by the architect himself to encourage urban public planning and architecture.

Further, Swaraj Art Archives is a vast family collection belonging to the art patron Vijay Kumar Aggarwal, which comprises books, prints, paintings, vintage China and cut glass, range of other artefacts and antiques. While Hoskote draws upon religious collections of the Museum of Christian Art, he also borrowed Christian portraits by Angelo da Fonseca from the intimate collections of Leonard and Naomi Menezes. This, for me, remains the most exciting aspect of the exhibition curation—the assemblage of art from disparate sources with varying ownerships and intent, carefully perceived and arranged to string together a narrative of cultural syncretism that interrogate and proves false many political agendas.

Notes

[1] Ranjit Hoskote and Ilija Trojanow, *Confluences: Forgotten Histories from East and West* (New Delhi: Yoda Press, 2012), 4.

[2] Hoskote and Trojanow, *Confluences: Forgotten Histories from East and West*, 7.

[3] GN Devy, *After Amnesia: Tradition and Change in Indian Literary Criticism* (New Delhi: Orient Longman, 1995), Online PDF.

[4] Félix Guattari and Gilles Deleuze, *A Thousand Plateaus: Capitalism and Schizophrenia* (USA: University of Minnesota Press, 1987).

[5] Christopher Pinney, *Photos of the Gods: The Printed Image and Political Struggle in India* (London: Reaktion Books, 2004), 191.

[6] Pinney, "Photos of the Gods": *The Printed Image and Political Struggle in India*, 22.

[7] Charles Correa, "The Public, the Private, and the Sacred," *A Place in the Shade: The New Landscape & Other Essays* (India: Penguin Books India, 2010), 26-46.

[8] Correa, "The Public, the Private, and the Sacred," *A Place in the Shade: The New Landscape & Other Essays.*

[9] Kapila Vatsyayan, "Sastra and Prayoga: Marga and Desi; On conceptual frameworks of Indian culture," in *Religion and Society in Eastern India*, ed. G. C. Tripathi and H. Kulke (Bhubaneshwar: The Eschmann Memorial Fund, 1994).

[10] Henri Lefebvre, "Reflections on the Politics of Space," trans. Michael J Enders, *Antipode* 8, No.2 (1976): 31.

[11] Savia Viegas, "Painting the Madonna Brown," *Himal Southasia*, Issue August 2010

[12] Savia Viegas, *Angelo da Fonseka*: *Passion and Glory*, (Goa: Xavier Centre of Historical Research, 2012).

[13] Jacques Derrida, "Archive Fever: A Freudian Impression," trans. Eric Prenowitz, *Diacritics* 25, No. 2 (Summer, 1995): 12.

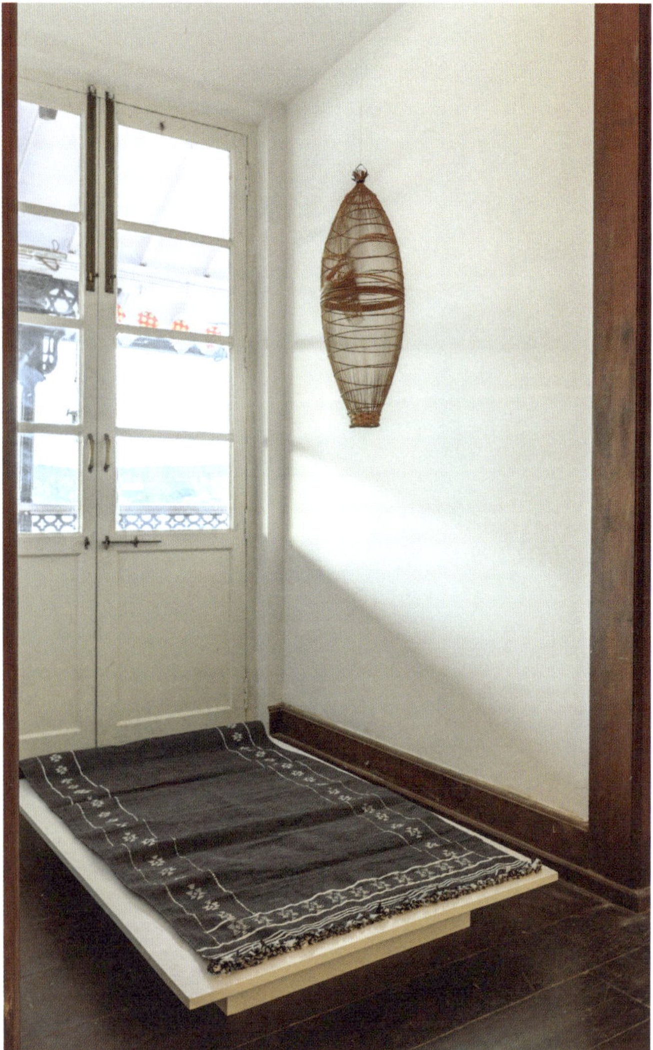

Taothum or *Kabo-Lu* (2018); Artisan unknown; Meitei-Pangal Community, Imphal Valley, Manipur; Bamboo, polythene cord

Chomukh Chatai (2018); Rajiben Murji Vankar; Recycled videotape plastic weft, plastic bags, nylon warp

Matters of Hand: Craft, Design and Technique

Curated by Rashmi Varma

Venue Adil Shah Palace

Curatorial Note

Exhibition Design *Reha Sodhi*
Collaborators *AKFD, Aman Khanna (Claymen), Avani, Chato Kuosto, Heirloom Naga, Ira Studio, Ishan Khosla, Jeenath Beevi, Kamli Devi & Jaipur Rugs Foundation, Meena Devi & Jaipur Rugs Foundation, Olivia Dar, Phantom Hands, Pio Coffrant & JIO Foundation, Rajiben Murji Vankar, Ramju Ali, Rooshad Shroff, Sandeep Sangaru, Senthil Kumar & Jaya Kumar, Shed, Suraj Prakash Maharana, Swapnaa Tamhane, Salemamad D. Khatri & Mukesh P. Prajapati, Tara Books, The Kishkinda Trust, Tiipoi, Venkataka Krishna, Yasanche and Zilu Kumbhar*
Special Thanks *Delhi Craft Council, Khamir, Gita Ram (Crafts Council of India), Poonam Verma, Mantu Charan, Vanita Varma, Malika Verma Kashyap and Paola Antonelli*
Curator *Rashmi Varma*

This exhibition venerated the handmade as experienced through objects of utility ranging from recent innovations to ubiquitous objects found in public and private spaces. *Matters of Hand: Craft, Design, and Technique* included objects such as kitchen utensils, storage, furniture, or lighting that are imbued with thought process and an aesthetic integrity that extend from the karigars/craftspeople/designers/artists/artisans themselves. The objects demonstrate that notions of 'craft' move along a continuum threaded into a dynamic past and a fast-approaching future. Whether an object has been in existence for millennia or created in our contemporary time, what was included in this exhibition exemplified a resistance to the ongoing discourse of modern vs. traditional that pervades handmade design. The hands, the eyes, the feet, or the movements of the human body are the primary tools for ingeniously transforming precious raw materials into objects drawn from the vast Indian landscape. The very essence of these natural, indigenous materials is integral to the design, such as the pliability of katlamara bamboo, the translucency of makrana marble, the sonorous rhythm of kansa bell metal, or the regional clays that transition from earth into burnt terracotta or milk white pottery. Environmental concerns and economic resources are further explored through the use of recycled materials, namely plastic and repurposed furniture that mirror the 21st century. Lost-wax casting, weaving, metal beating, marble carving, block printing, lathe-turning, embroidering or inlaying are some of the techniques employed. Geometry, symmetry, colour and texture reveal the inherent nature of these elegant forms and announce their presence in an increasingly homogenised world.

Some works included here had been realised through formal working relationships within a two-way system of knowledge-transfer between practitioners and other works made independently in urban and rural environments. A profound respect is shared for traditional modes of techniques and cultural expression; however some works are not driven by these methods and thereby push process and find new expression. Others adhere closer to ideas which have persisted throughout time and space demonstrating refinement and artistry, whist some objects were spontaneously designed from a lack of resources.

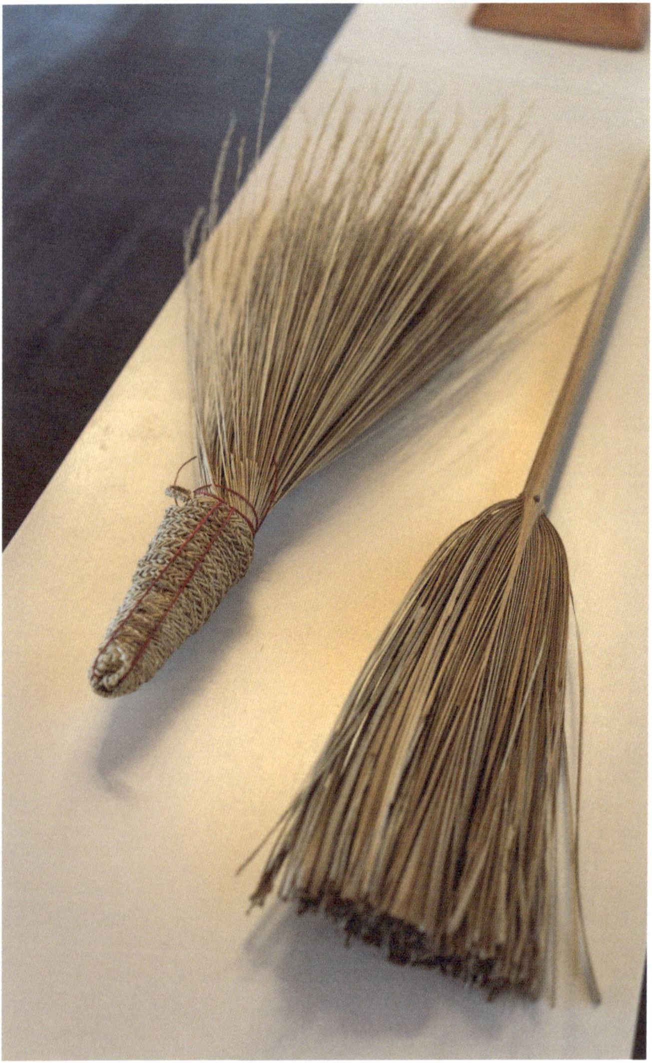

Serakipharo (2018); Artisan unknown; Nagaland; Palm leaf

Jharu (2018); Artisan unknown; Jharkhand; Grass

On Matters of Hand: Craft, Design and Technique

SKYE ARUNDHATI THOMAS

In a high-vaulted room on the top floor of the Adil Shah Palace, with large windows that open out to Goa's smoothly blue Mandovi river, designer Rashmi Varma has placed a pair of handmade household brooms on a long white table, under an enormous crystal chandelier. The chandelier's ostentatious extravagance is met by the clean curvature of the grass and date leaf brooms: finely wound together to create a unique geometry, braided and rolled for the appropriate width and base, different leaves joined by delicately placed knots and pins. With this simple juxtaposition, Varma erases the hierarchies implied between the objects, and the histories that sustain them. "Each object is a social environment as well as an economic one," she says as we move through *Matters of Hand: Craft, Design and Technique*, her curated show at Serendipity Arts Festival 2018, for which she has carefully brought together objects from across India that reflect a certain formal sensibility. "I am trying to move away from strict definitions of 'traditional' or 'modern'," Varma adds as we pause in front of the brooms, "things have been modern for over 5,000 years."

At the entrance of the show are a series of mended objects: two stools, a chair, two lifeguard chairs and a sculpture from the collection of designer Ishan Khosla. The chairs and stools, part of a series entitled *Construct Deconstruct Construct* (2018), are most often sourced from public spaces, and have been repeatedly repaired by using scraps and pieces of plastic, rope, metal, wood, leaves, twine and cloth. Here, form is spontaneous, as is the process of making. The more you pay attention, the more the objects reveal their details: a plastic tarpaulin twisted into a piece of palm leaf and yellow rope to fix a broken roof, or a staggered set of nails bent together to secure the broken limb of a stool. Khosla finds that "these vernacular pieces of furniture are gestural in nature ... the sitter and the seat are reflections of each other, they both represent the beauty of imperfection." By opening the show with these pieces, Varma seems to set the tone for the show—the premise here is to pay attention. She is less interested in objects that are beautiful, and more in those that are complex and full of history.

A sense of quiet pervades through the show, allowing for the geometry and internal rhythms of the objects to speak for themselves. Varma's chosen objects lend easily to abstraction: each has a certain rudimentary form or pattern of repetition which, when isolated, can still stand on its own, without requiring additional embellishments. Narratives around Indian craft often veer toward an excess of a decorative saturation of colour, motif and symbol. Varma shows us that the opposite can be true. In one corner sits a set of simple and smoothly spun pottery vessels: a *bhadak* and *bhabbhu* for water, a *maati* for churning buttermilk, a *paatar* for kneading dough and a *karsiyo* for drinking water or setting yoghurt. These come from Kutch, Western Gujarat, from a stoneware making practice that finds its roots all the way back to the Indus Valley Civilisation.

Varma brings in the pottery of the *kumbhar* Ramju Ali, who imbues each object with an uncomplicated but highly specific shape, using many different techniques. These objects are hand formed and beaten using a *faraai*, a flat wooden paddle. To soften the clay before working with it, Ali kneads it with his feet for about an hour, pummeling and massaging it to get the right consistency. Each object is then appropriately pinched, thrown or coiled according to the nature of its use. Some pots are later painted with a gossamer white pigment in flowing lines of fish, waves and hatches, which are characteristic of Kutchi pottery. Around the *bhadak* is a red cording—almost like a tight, knitted sweater—made by Ali's son Ahmed, which protects the pot from breaking and from the sweltering rays of the sun. Ramju Ali is especially attentive in making pottery for the *aam admi*: he protects the vessels from wear and tear so that farmers can carry them out into the fields without worry. Although certain craft items make it to urban environments under expensive labels or handloom fairs, many are still in use in a local, regional way, as Ali's practice shows.

Elsewhere in the room, a *korai* grass *pais* or mat—known in its home state of Tamil Nadu as *pattu pais* after the town Pattamadai, where it has been made for generations—softly shimmers in tones of a dusty-golden pink and beige, where a small floral, but highly geometric, pattern repeats itself endlessly in an almost dizzyingly perfect symmetry. The mat sits soft and pliable, appearing as though made of woven fabric. Where such weaving is most often done with dry material, in Pattamadai, the Labbai and Rowther, communities split korai grass into fine strips and wet these with water from the Thamirabarani River (traditionally named Tamaraparani), upon whose banks the grass usually grows. Horizontal bands of colour are carefully woven together, with cotton or nylon in the warp. Patterns for the mats are usually inspired by sari designs, or the parallel lines of Bhavani dhurries, geometric blankets woven from a coarse thread called *jamakkalam*.

The *pattu pais* is no ordinary mat. As Pushpa Chari writes for *The Hindu* (1996):

> In the metamorphosis of the green korai growing wild on the banks of the Tamaraparani, into the wonder that is the Pattamadai mat lies the genius of the *paramparic* [traditional] Indian craftsman ... his empathy with the moods and rhythms of nature ... as well as total dedication to his calling spells the very essence of India's craft heritage, be it the *minakari* and *jadau* jewellery of Jaipur, the *namdahs* and carpets of Kashmir, the shola pith craft of Bengal or the stone carvings of Karnataka.[1]

Chari draws a landscape from which to view the mats: they belong to an ancient industry of tools, mechanisms and community. Like the brooms under a crystal chandelier, the mats are as precious as Jaipur gems. For the mat displayed in *Matters of Hand*, its creator and designer, Jeenath Beevi, who is part of a generations-old weaving family in Pattamadai, wove in an elegant *mullai poo*: a small jasmine bud motif. The highest quality of *pattu pais* is so intricate and silky that it sits at the equivalent of 120 thread counts. Mats like these often accompany a bride to her new home, and may bear the names of the wedded couple at the top. Beevi has added the word "serendipity" for this particular occasion.

Varma's reluctance to define practices as "traditional" or "modern" is useful, and important. Craft often lends itself to a nationalistic discourse—both historically and in the present day—as it often becomes a manner by which to uphold misplaced notions of "authenticity." What feels important here is that craft does not belong to a geography, it belongs to movement and migration. What is often implied by the term tradition is that it is immutable, or has remained unchanged over time. A tradition is, of course, the opposite of this: it is hybrid, dynamic and ever evolving, especially for craft, where techniques and process are the evidence of decades-long exchanges between different individuals, infrastructure and communities. Varma's own design practice is deeply rooted in materiality and technique, informed by her travels through the subcontinent and a careful attention to the craft proficiencies of different regions and mediums. For *Matters of Hand*, she has travelled extensively, familiarising herself with not only the objects themselves, but the communities and families that have been involved in making them for generations.

A particularly striking moment in this regard is a video whose sound fills up the room with a rhythmic tapping. In it, a group of about eight men beat a piece of metal at highly coordinated and methodical intervals. In the small video taken by Varma at the workshop of Suraj Prakash Maharana—from the Kansari community of Kantilo, Odisha—a group of craftsmen under his employ work on a *kansa* disc.

Kansa is a bell-metal alloy made from a mix of 85% copper and 5% tin, properties that Ayurveda considers to play an important role in the body's metabolism by providing a gradual release of iron, which in turn eliminates free radicals and kills bacteria. To make the kansa discs, which operate as a raw material for what eventually becomes household utensils, molten alloy is poured into terracotta moulds that have been first rubbed with mustard oil. From the moulds, small circular ingots are leaked out and hand beaten by a group of artisans into required shapes. Their choreography is like a dance, one of a primal kind—ceremonial, and in a tight circular fist around an open fire. By isolating this one element of the process through film, Varma amplifies its meditative quality. The Kansari artisans begin the metalwork in the early hours of the morning, before dawn, while the day is still cool, and work till noon.

The disc is kept over an open fire to remain malleable enough to be beaten into shape, and the term "bell-metal" alludes to the musical sounds of the tapping on the hot disc. The metal is shaped into plates, bowls and other utensils, the finishing process for which requires a grinding (both by machine and hand) to smoothen out and polish the toughened metal. The kansa utensils are enormously heavy, given their composition, and can often weigh up to two or three kilograms a piece. Each is a nearly black matte, or otherwise polished to a rich, golden hue. The metal is almost glassy, as though dipped in reflective oil. At *Matters of Hand*, a set of utensils from Maharana's workshop is placed underneath the video. They are more slender and lightweight than conventional kansa utensils, as he has devised a method by which to reduce their overall weight, giving him a competitive edge at a time when ultra-light stainless steel and aluminum are all but replacing this ancient craft.

As is so dramatically illustrated by the video from Maharana's workshop, there is something innately ritualistic and performative to the crafts of the subcontinent. As Partha Mitter writes in *Art and Nationalism in Colonial India, 1850 – 1922: Occidental Orientations* (1994), the ancient arts of the subcontinent are "living traditions of

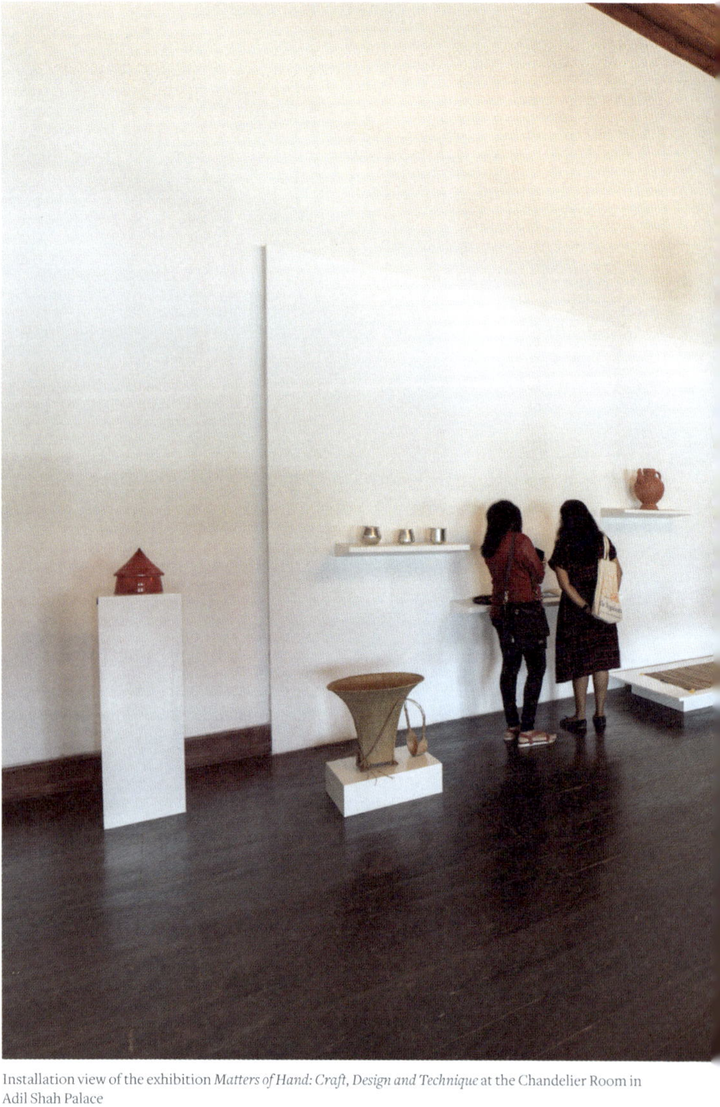

Installation view of the exhibition *Matters of Hand: Craft, Design and Technique* at the Chandelier Room in Adil Shah Palace

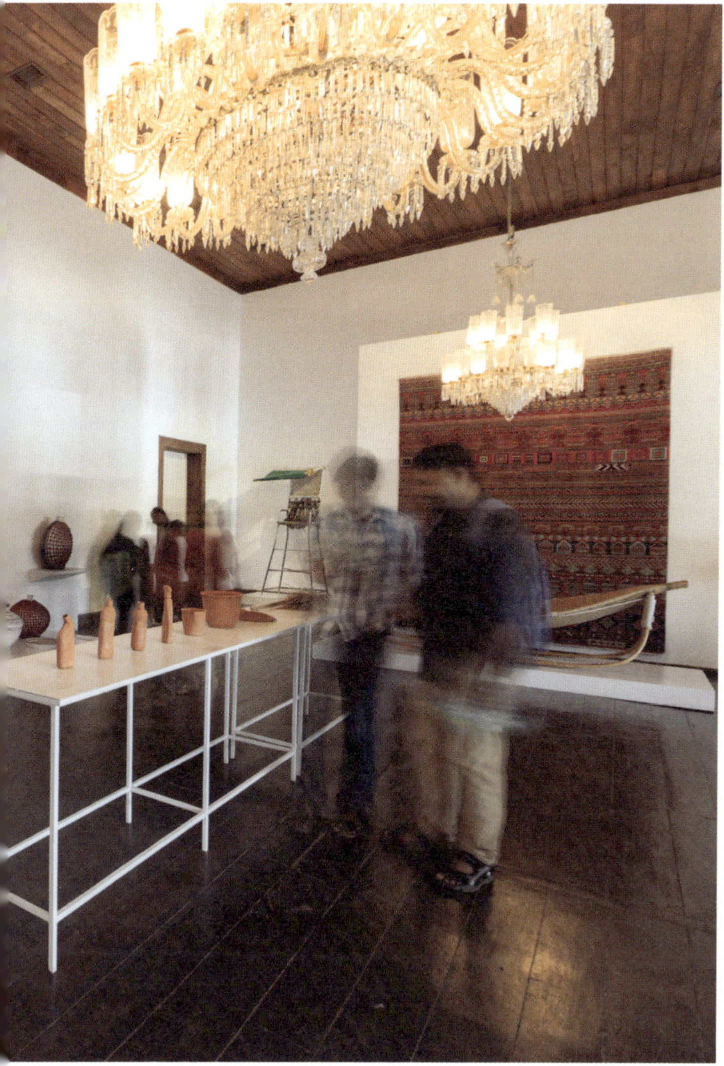

craftsmanship."[2] We may read into them as almost utopian spaces in which identity, community and even protest are performed through ritual and labour. Where Western notions of craft often relegate form, technique and invention to individual makers, in India these are almost always about community. However, it is crucial that this very notion of community is critically examined. In the subcontinent, it is impossible to speak about community, craft, skill or tradition without a discussion of caste, and this is especially true of practices where generations of the same communities have been making the same object, or working with the same material.

Usually, kinship, caste and occupational ties bind craft communities. These are often governed by the Jajmani system: a pre-industrial socio-economic system in which lower castes are tied to certain labour practices (and monetary remittances) by upper caste landlords or traders. The etymology of the word Jamjani traces back to *yajman*, a word for patron. However, the realities of these relationships are not nearly as polite; they are considered an almost permanent hierarchy, not based on any written contract, but solely on caste. It is thus essential to continuously remember that in India, the material and labour relations of technique, production and exchange are completely inextricable from the internal structures of caste. In an effort toward transparency, Varma has at every instance explicitly mentioned the community that is involved with each object.

What caste does, apart from its obviously violent segregations, is make these skills entirely oral histories: it is not as though these techniques and forms find other translations, or are shared between castes; they are instead passed on between members of the same caste and community. This makes them even more fragile and susceptible to erasure, particularly under industrialisation and the introduction of new materials, or the loss of older material palettes.

For the Martiniquan postcolonial scholar Édouard Glissant, "History (with a capital *H*) ends where the histories of those people once reputed to be without history come together."[3] In his seminal 1976 essay "The Quarrel with History," Glissant articulates an insightful argument in which he deconstructs the histories of the various colonisations of the Caribbean countries, and the patterns of slavery that arose as a result. There is of course a much broader link, and his essay may begin to inform a critique on the writing of the histories of the Indian subcontinent as well. For Glissant, it is the artefacts of culture, literature, architecture, music and art, that we must use in the building of a new narrative, one that can divorce itself from its mainstream counterpart as a way to maintain a "continuous, open resistance" against hegemonic knowledge structures.[4] History, written flatly, with a linear arc of progression, can reduce things to chronology, where events are highlighted for their exceptional quality. Whereas it is in oral traditions that we may begin to construct more complex, nuanced and robust narratives. To extend Glissant's concerns, we must also have a critical reflection on the histories of craft, and the communities that have mobilised its practices.

"Craft," in the manner by which we use it today, was first put to use in late eighteenth-century Britain,[5] moving to different parts of the world in the nineteenth. This movement was a result of empire, where nineteenth-century British thinkers were preoccupied by concerns that brought both the vernacular and decorative arts together with the politics of labour, as proposed by Paul Greenhalgh in "The History of Craft" (1997). This was the direct result of a growing anxiety towards industrialisation, which in turn led to an increased attention, and even valorisation, of the vernacular. It was important to go back to village life, to the countryside craftspeople, and (in what is trickier territory) "the authentic tradition." At the same time, the decorative arts (or these so-called authentic traditions) were being separated from the fine arts, which were growing to be an exclusive category under the thrust of modernity. Incidentally, the resistance to mechanical means of production goes back to the Industrial Revolution, where figures like John Ruskin and William Morris wrote of alienated labourers in the machine age (as is evident in their writings around the nineteenth-century British Arts and Crafts Movement), and produced long theses that romanticised non-industrial work. Incidentally,

Morris took up the cause of protecting Indian artisans from the aggressive tools of industrialisation. Thus, under the British-led Arts and Crafts Movement of the 1850s, vernacular traditions, politics of labour and decorative arts were flung together to coin the term "craft." As Greenhalgh writes, "the historical moment was right, the combination in this context dynamic and compelling."[6]

In the Indian context, the vernacular became a tool to defeat empire. The Quit India Movement, launched in 1942, appropriated and drew from the language of the farmer and country labourer in order to resist the mechanisms of empire, and with it, to initiate an early legacy of closed market economics. The socialist concerns of the new republic were immediate: the labourer could no longer remain alienated by the economy or politics. In the fine arts, modernist thinkers and painters began a long preoccupation with the pastoral and the vernacular: looking to the countryside for motif, symbol and metaphor. Traditions were seen as something to be updated and infused with the modernist sensibility of a young republic. The separations between the crafts and fine arts remained, although many artists dabbled in the abstraction of multiple craft motifs, reproducing them on their canvases or through sculpture.

Greenhalgh also writes that craft is "a signifier that has no stable significance."[7] He implies that from the very inception of the word, nobody knows what to do about it. What history seems to show us is that the term collectively describes and flattens separate genres that were not always placed together in any category. And most importantly: where each grows from completely separate circumstances. This could not be truer than in the Indian subcontinent, where as Varma's skilful curation shows, many objects produce a very specific function according to their forms and material.

Varma also brings into a space that functions much like a white cube, objects that are neither conceptual nor figurative—they simply exist as they are—allowing the viewer to rest eyes on formal symmetries and functions. What is most refreshing about her rooms at the Adil

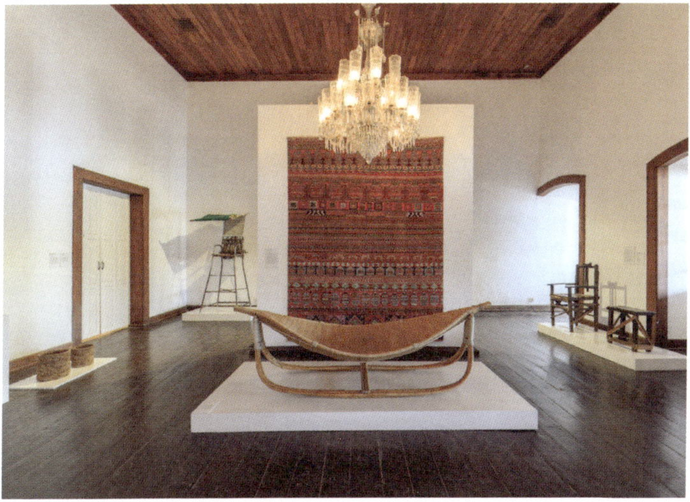

Mess Is More (2018); Aman Khanna, Bhoop Singh, Gyan Chiluvery, Shankar Singh; Terracotta clay

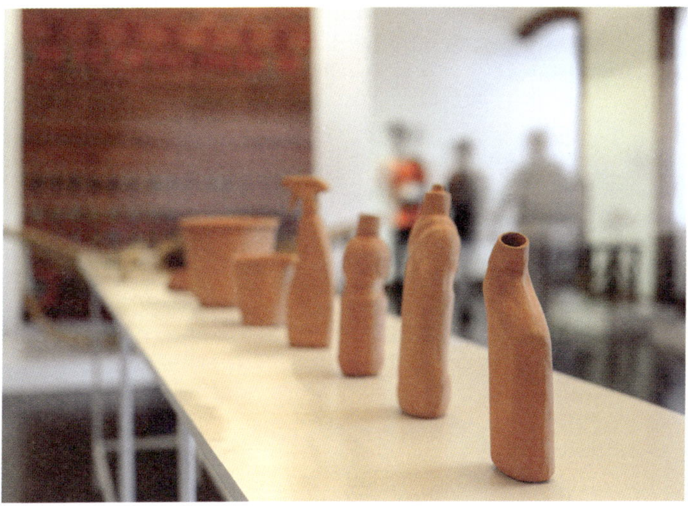

Lounger (2013); Yashesh Virkar; Bamboo, cotton cord

Shah Palace is the stillness and space that is afforded to each object.

You are drawn to their surfaces, textures and forms. You pay attention to the slightest graduations in colour: in *Kalash* (2016), a rug from the Manchaha series of the Jaipur Rug Foundation, subtle graduations of shade and hue softly dabble in the light. The rug was created by Kamli Devi, and assisted by her friend Bimla Devi— artisans who otherwise work with the company Jaipur Rugs on predetermined designs for commercial sales. However, in the Manchaha (which roughly translates to "as your mind desires") series, the artisans were given free rein to create their own designs for rugs, the only constraint being the colour palette they could use. It was an initiative with the intention to use the excess stock yarn left over from commercial production. Devi was given hues of red and pink, and she in turn made an intricate tapestry of ceremonial vessels, snacks, doors, diamonds and symbols for good luck. There is never a moment where the colour is flat or unified. Given the limited quantities for each shade, Devi continuously blends colours together, much like an oil painter working on a single panel for months in different shades. At *Matters of Hand*, it's not always about what the eye is able to see, but also what the eye might find soothing, enticing or drawn to focus on for an extended period of time. There is a meditative quality to looking, in the same way that there is a meditation in the making.

While there are works that are soothing to the eye, there are also those that are physical architectures and are soothing to *be* in. These are also works that are largely conceptual but turn functional quite easily; for example, in Swapnaa Tamhane's soft architecture in *Tent: A space for the ceremony of close readings* (2018), at any given moment of the day, people could be seen resting, whispering, giggling or sharing an intimate moment. Inspired by the mid-1950s Mill Owner's Association Building designed by Le Corbusier and Balkrishna Doshi in Ahmedabad, Gujarat, Tamhane designed a series of block prints that repeat endlessly on a flowing cotton khadi structure that is tacked up on a metal frame, and affixed with tassels. She uses details from the facade of the building, the inner conference room and the

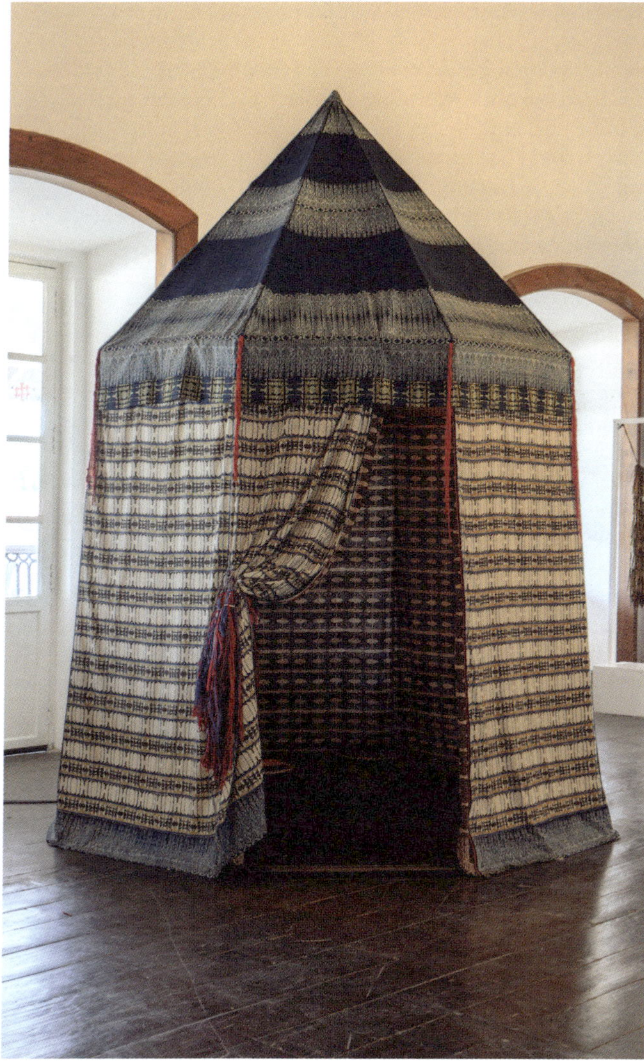

Tent: A space for the ceremony of close readings (2018); Swapnaa Tamhane, Mukesh P. Prajapti, Salehmamad D. Khatri; Cotton, natural dyes, metal frame, handmade paper lantern, tassels

roof to draw up her block prints. Inside the tent hangs a small paper lantern that Tamhane has handmade, using mulched khadi cotton, and with a cutout that repeats the same design. The blocks used for printing were carved by Mukesh P. Prajapati in Petaphur, and the cotton khadi fabric dyed by Salehmamad D. Khatri of Ajrakhpur, Kutch, Gujarat. This particular block-printing process was no simple task: it required scouring, lime resist printing, mordanting and dyeing the cloth multiple times to produce the right tone and colour. Tamhane's soft architecture is both cosy and grand: with a swooped ceiling and diffused light.

"I think my favourite parts of the travels were meeting with the families of the different artisans, eating with them and spending time," Varma tells me as we sit out on the balcony of the Adil Shah Palace. It's a blazing day and the sun is shining hard off the glistening Mandovi as she speaks, a vivid backdrop against which she tells me her stories and details of the objects on display (which most often turn into anecdotes about their makers). Varma is thoughtful and gentle in a manner that is completely charming, and it is at once clear that she has poured a lot of herself into this show, which is a portrait of the forms that she is drawn to and the collaborations that are meaningful to her. "The family is very much part of the craft," she adds, "and it is hard to separate the life from the work."

I look out onto the river as large ferries trudge across its length and illuminated signboards flicker over at the opposite bank with ads for casinos and beer. A shining patch in the water catches my eye and I watch as a single plastic bottle scurries its way along with the tide, an image that stays with me as I walk back into *Matters of Hand*. Every single object in here could be replaced, or has already been, replaced by plastic, I think, shuddering internally. I quickly return to one of my favourite pieces from the show, *Chomukh Chatai* (2018) by Rajineb Murji Vankar: a mat made from recycled videocassette tape, plastic bags and nylon wrap. Vankar is also from Kutch, where the most ubiquitous method of waste disposal is burning large piles of plastic and trash, releasing heady toxins into the night air. In an initiative started by the non-profit organisation Khamir, plastic waste collectors (of the lower castes) were employed and properly contracted to collect, sort and strip the raw materials for weavers to weave out intricate and durable textiles. Nylon is used for the warp, plastic for the weft and the weaves created on pit looms that are ancient to the region. The thick material is then crafted into backpacks, cushions, mats, wallpaper and coverings. In "Chomukh Chatai," Vankar has created a vibrant tableau of floral geometric motifs (*chomukh*) with white plastic bags, complemented by the glassy blacks of videocassette film. The work takes me to the desert and to the Kutchi salt flats, frozen in my memory with similarly satin textures of sand and salt.

Notes

[1] P. Chari, "The wonder of the Pattamadai mat," *The Hindu*, February 25, 1996,15.

[2] Partha Mitter, *Art and Nationalism in Colonial India, 1850-1922: Occidental Orientations* (New York: Columbia University Press, 1995).

[3] Édouard Glissant, "The Quarrel with History," in *Caribbean Discourse: Selected Essays,* trans. by J. Michael Dash (Charlottesville & London: University of Virginia Press, 1989), 64.

[4] Glissant, "The Quarrel with History," 63.

[5] Paul Greenhalgh, "The History of Craft," in *The Culture of Craft,* ed. Peter Dormer (Minneapolis, Manchester: Manchester University Press, 1997), 20.

[6] Greenhalgh, "The History of Craft," 35.

[7] Greenhalgh, "The History of Craft," 20-21.

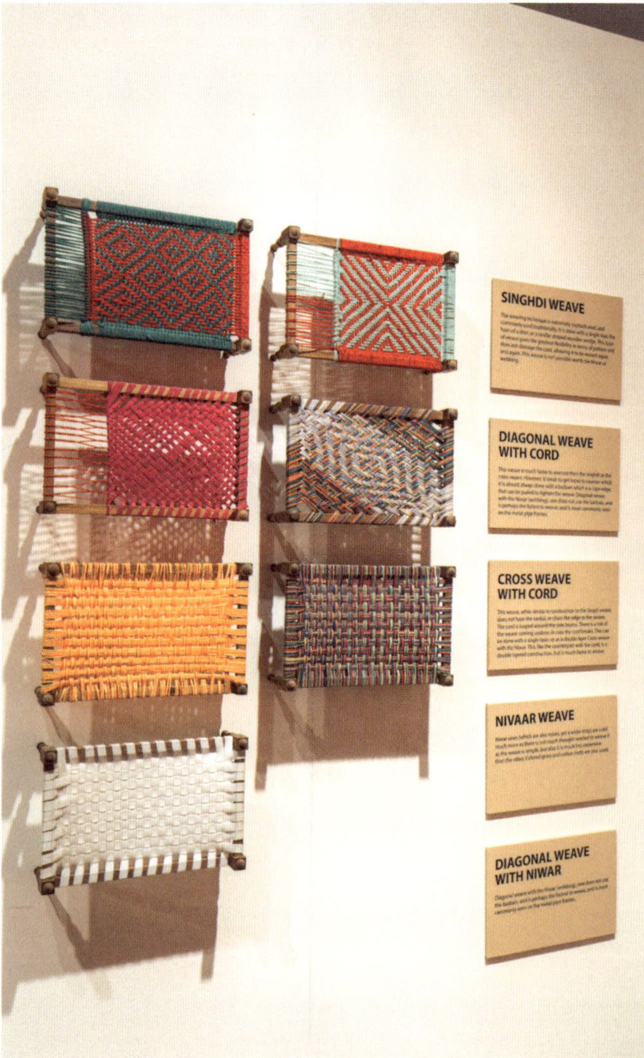

Detail of *The Charpai* installation view displaying different weaves on miniature charpais

The Charpai

Curated by Ayush Kasliwal

Venue Adil Shah Palace & The Art Park

Curatorial Note

Curatorial Assistant *Ramayudh Sahu*
Collaborators *AKFD Studio, Hem Singh, Poona Ram, Indi Store, Retyrement Plan, Bijoy Jain and Narendra Bhawan*
Special Thanks *Association of Designers of India, Design Innovation & Craft Resource Centre (DRIC), Indian School of Design & Innovation (Mumbai), Creaticity (Pune), CEPT University (Ahmedabad), IICD (Jaipur), Pearl Academy (Delhi), Dr. Skye Morrison, Anand Belhe, Rashmi Ranade and Darpana Athale*
Special Project Curator *Ayush Kasliwal*

If one were to imagine a single piece of furniture that is truly Indian, it would be the *charpai*. The charpai is a rectangular wooden frame having four legs (hence the word char pai), with a woven fiber/fabric as the surface. It is used across the Indian subcontinent, particularly in the hot and relatively dry regions of Rajasthan, Gujarat and Maharashtra. The variant in the wet climates has a solid wooden surface. The project aimed to explore the charpai from a historic and cultural point of view, and simultaneously carry it into the future by inviting leading thinkers and designers to interpret the charpai, and present it at the festival. The thematic extension of the charpai was achieved by placing them in multiple locations, positioning them in creative ways, thereby encouraging use as well as recognition of the charpai as furniture that is relevant and unique to India.

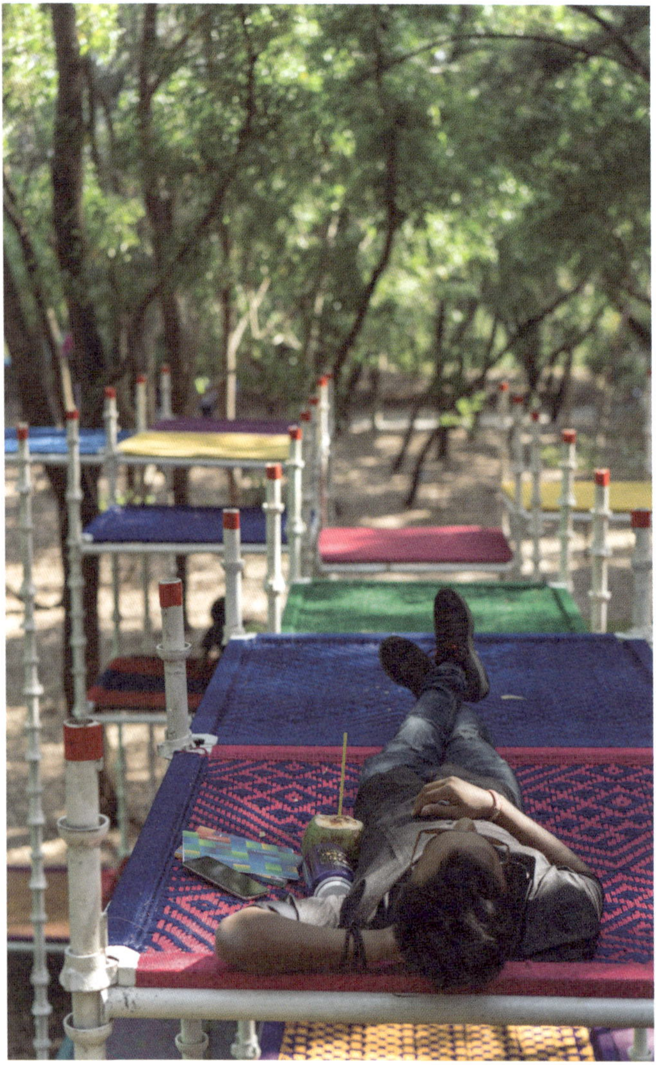

Scenes from *The Charpai* installation at The Children's (Art) Park

The Charpai Project

BHARATHY SINGARAVEL

The Charpai Project, curated by Ayush Kasliwal for Serendipity Arts Festival 2018, strives to dislodge the idea of the traditional day-bed, used across the Indian subcontinent, as only a piece of furniture that may or may not be in popular use today. Kasliwal is certainly keen on enabling a resurgence of the *charpai,* both in design practice and in its usage. The project desires to reflect the nature of the charpai and its versatility. This small-scale show, in one of the recesses of the Adil Shah Palace, engages with the charpai as a site, a rupture in conventional (or enforced) concepts of private and public space, a reservoir of knowledge, cultural practices, historical migration and as a symbol. For the curator, the charpai is at once frugal in design and yet, versatile—this idea is an essential curatorial element. As a designer, he questions the drive for the "new" and "different" that gripes design practices. A basic charpai's material requirements are unassuming and, in his view, it is easy to learn how to weave one. Kasliwal chose to prove this by running charpai-making workshops in different design colleges. He explains:

> Very often the dialogue in the world of design is "How different is it?" I would challenge that. Is "different" the qualifier for design? Why this obsession with the new? Are we so scared of who we are, that we constantly try to reinvent ourselves? Do we need to? Or do we need to step back a little and instead of saying "let's do things differently," say "let's do things better? Let's do things which are more intelligent." Especially, given that we live in the tropics, we will be the first victims of climate change and if anything has to be done, we have to do it. I know it is a very wide thing that I'm trying

> to address. One sees just an object, but all these things come together in this project. Our belief structures and how we think the future can pan out if we choose it to be so.

For Kasliwal, one solution is to fall back, when possible, on items that traditionally have a more sustainable method of production. Frugality suggests to him, maybe a little idealistically, a requisite mind-set in a world hurtling towards disastrous climate-change outcomes. While conversations around climate change and sustainability occur across the globe, Kasliwal feels it is up to us to take initiative. *The Charpai Project* is a formula that could provide a learning curve towards a more sustainable future. "If we can have a bed that we can lift up and put on the side, it means that we can have smaller homes," he hopes. I am of a sceptical bent of mind and can't help wondering if an entire section of the global population's desire for excesses can be curbed so easily.

Kasliwal describes the actual process by which a charpai comes together as ideal. On most occasions, these structures are not found as ready-made. One can source the frame from a carpenter, source the rope, and then find a person who can do the weaving at a price—the charpai's ecosystem, as he calls it. This he chose to indicate by requiring viewers to enter the exhibition via a "shop" where one encounters unravelled charpais, frames, and coils of rope and tape.

'THE CHARPAI IN TIME'[1] AND SPACE

It is a fairly obvious conclusion to arrive at that this frugality in design enabled the charpai's portability. Apart from making it easy to store and move around, the charpai appears to have travelled to Sudan, and along the western coast of the African continent through trade routes.[2] Sikhs enlisted by the British for their police forces in Malaysia carried the charpai with them.[3] Similar to borders, knowledge and tradition tend to be porous, and the charpai found an iteration of itself that was both local and rooted in its origin in the subcontinent. Jay Thakker, Director of the Design Innovation and Craft Resource

Centre (DICRC) at CEPT University, Ahmedabad, addressed this in conversation with me. For Jay, who is one of the authors of *Sahaj: Vernacular Furniture of Gujarat* (2018), a publication by CEPT University Press that the *Charpai Project* draws research material from, the charpai's multiplicity is only an extension of indigenous concepts of space in general. The charpai can be a space unto itself, belonging to a single individual; it can also be a gathering place, or somewhere to dry spices—versatile in its uses, because the idea of designating living spaces into dining quarters or bedrooms itself is alien, he explains.

This is not to say that different types of social structures and hierarchies are not applicable. The *dholio*, a Gujarati charpai of hefty turned-wood legs and red lacquer finish, is traditionally a male space. To be invited to sit on it is a signal of extending equal status. The dholio is burnt along with its owner at his funeral pyre.[4] The field researchers at the DICRC found that in the case the owner had died and been cremated elsewhere, the rebuying of the abandoned dholio was taboo. Similarly, *Sahaj: Vernacular Furniture of Gujarat*, released following extensive research primarily in Gujarat, Rajasthan, and Punjab, also claims that men from well-to-do families are given a charpai at birth and are carried to their funeral pyres on it. The dholio is given away to low-income families after the cremation. Both practices seem to be followed with the former perhaps pre-dating the latter. It is important to draw attention to the larger practice across the country of "donating" the deceased's possessions to oppressed castes and the socio-political implications that go with it.

The researchers and writers also came across "feminine" counterparts to the dholio called a *dholini*, which has slender and more ornamental legs, and tends to be used by all members of the family. The publication itself can be referred to for further knowledge on varying social practices concerning these charpais across communities and the structural differences among the types of charpai.

Given that in our present context, where a bed is commonly the centrepiece of the most private space in the house, the charpai dodges such fixed functionality. Particularly in its rural lifespan, the charpai is neither viewed as an outdoor object nor a specifically indoor one—it is both. Kasliwal brings up how, "we in our cities have a very strict line of what is inside and outside, what is ours and not ours, what is private and what is shared." To him this is an indicator of the need to address the "tragedy of the commons," a condition of shared resources first discussed in the context of cattle grazing by the mathematician William Foster Loyd in 1833, and made widely known by the ecologist Garrett Hardin in 1968. Hardin was referring to a set of problems that he termed "no technical solution problems,"[5] and his basic contention was with how the crisis of over-population was being addressed. He argued that the tendency to try and resolve this crisis by "farming the seas or developing new strains of wheat"[6] through technology was impossible. Responses to Hardin's theory have been undertaken in social sciences for decades, which I'm not equipped to bring in here. But what does intrigue me however, is Kasliwal's curatorial linking of Hardin's views to his own misgivings about the "loss of the commons." He explains: "It becomes abjectly clear that India suffers from that; the charpai is about the commons, about shared spaces and I personally can't associate the two concepts since Hardin was advocating for intensive regulation of what he refers to as the commons and also 'relinquishing the freedom to breed.'"

When Kasliwal discussed the many uses of the charpai it became clear that it is highly adaptable. We agreed that it was because of this, that at the heart of the exhibition was the making of an object that fit into daily requirements and social structures. Along with easy portability was its requisite adaptability. I introduce a degree of whimsy here. In contrast (or can it be in companionship?) to the aforementioned ritualism concerning the dholio, is an anecdote about Ismat Chughtai. Nilanjana S. Roy, in an article written for *Business Standard* titled "A Charpai of Her Own," quotes Saadat Hasan Manto writing on Chughtai. The following passage seems to suggest that perhaps the charpai is first and foremost, a self-contained place:

> "Ismat had this habit of chewing ice. She would hold a piece in her hand and crunch on it noisily. She would be lying down on the charpai supported by her elbow, with her notebook open before her on the pillow. She would hold a fountain pen in one hand and a chunk of ice in the other. The radio would go on blaring, but Ismat's pen would race along on the paper with a gentle rustle as her teeth smashed the ice to pieces." Over time, the "gentle rustle" of the pen on the paper would give way to a steady flow—Ismat would write "not caring about her spelling or the use of diacritical marks," or anything except the need to capture the quicksilver images in her mind. But what struck me was the space that Ismat occupied—small but absolute, a charpai of her own, in answer to Virginia Woolf's dictum that a woman writer must have a room of her own.

For Chughtai, surrounded by a family's needs and household, as Roy illustrates, the charpai was at once a sanctuary and a barrier. The barricades of class, caste and gender identity on the other hand that informs the ritualisms, do in my opinion require sensitive critique as much as it provides for intriguing research material. However, with regard to such hierarchies, the curator and I have different views. I believe that identifying hierarchies both structural and insidious, is a necessary part of research. To me, even from the two anecdotes mentioned here, two opposing ideas of the charpai come together—conflicted, but co-existing; one engaging with identity built on caste and gender, and the other built upon the spaces claimed by the modern feminist.

If social structures/hierarchies do have a relevance, what happens when the charpai finds itself in entirely new markets?

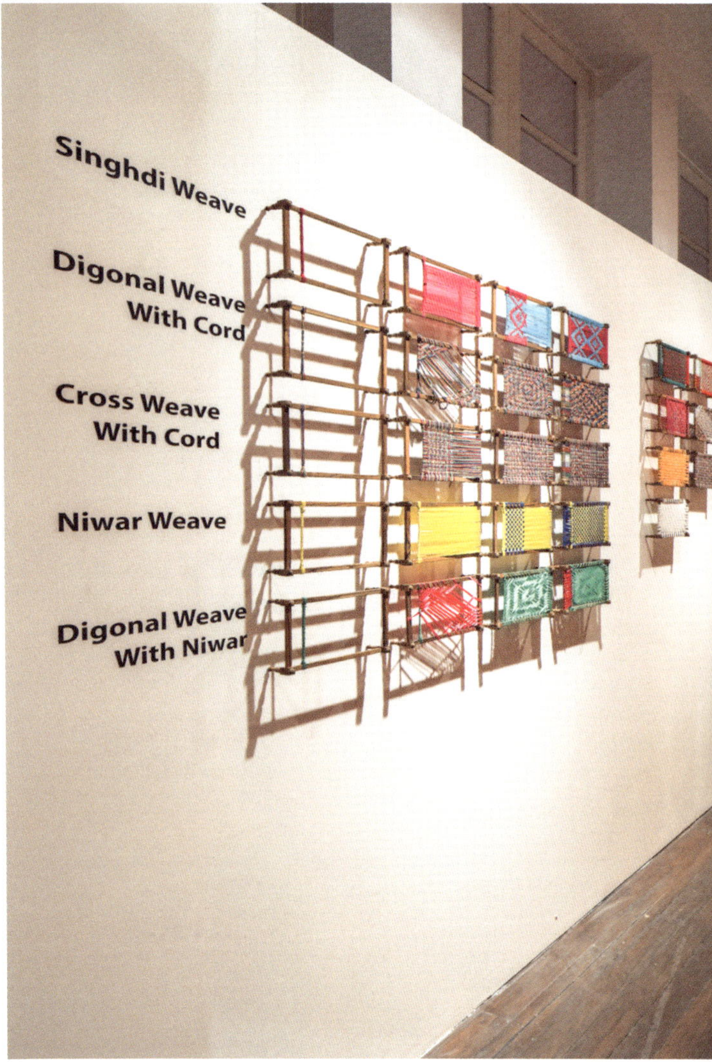

Installation view from *The Charpai*

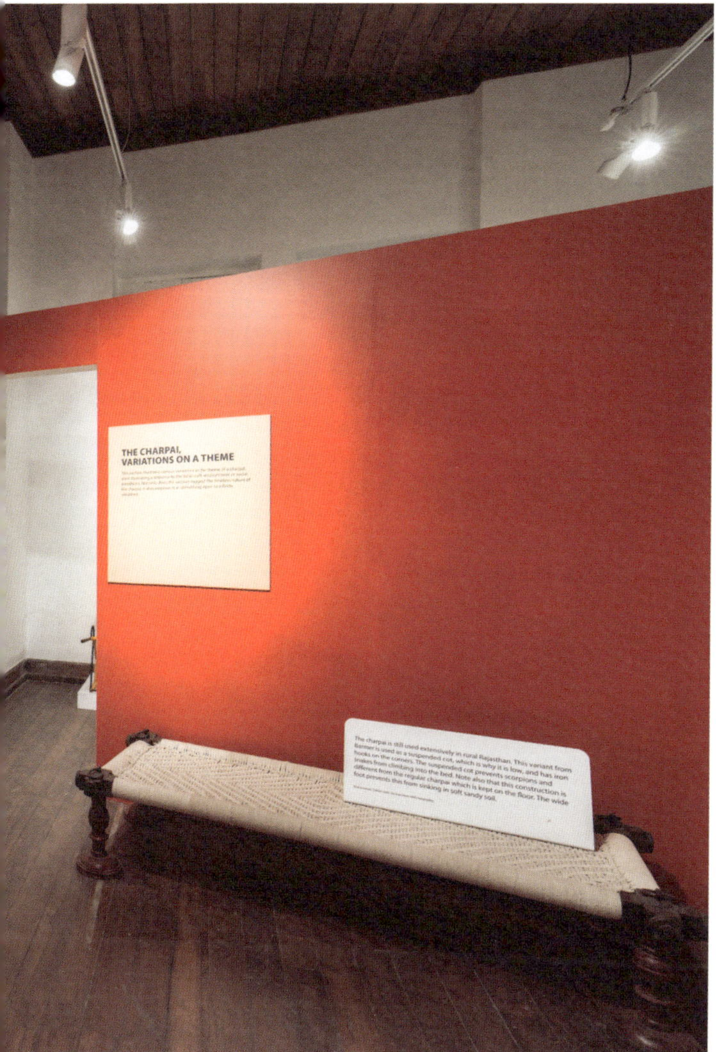
THE CHARPAI, VARIATIONS ON A THEME
The charpai is still used extensively in rural Rajasthan. This variant from Barmer is used as a suspended cot, which is why it is low, and has iron hooks on the corners. The suspended cot prevents scorpions and snakes from climbing into the bed. Note also that this construction is different from the regular charpai which is kept on the floor. The wide foot prevents this from sinking in soft sandy soil.

ASSIMILATION VS. APPROPRIATION: IS THE QUEST FOR REVIVALISM AND RELEVANCE TO BE AN UNREGULATED UNDERTAKING?

The charpai, as mentioned before, has travelled beyond the subcontinent and therefore assimilated into other cultures and forms. Additionally, the actual need of the day-bed, as Jay Thakker pointed out to me, may have simultaneously evolved across the world. However, one of the issues that confront the *Charpai Project* is the question of "relevance." In this regard, I'm unclear as to what the benchmark for this is. Discussions around something having to be made relevant again commence, and so begins a project of revivalism. Is the charpai truly disappearing, and in whose context does it need to witness resurgence? Certainly, rural Indian living spaces and the rules that govern them continue to change. Social mobility (or the desire for it) brings items and trends that may be classified as alien. Kasliwal mentioned that during his trips to old Jaipur, he realised that the scale of the havelis sat rather incongruously with the objects that have come to occupy them. A hulking double bed and a dressing table placed along the walls of a room take up far more space than a charpai that would have been brought to the marital home by a new bride ever could. Class signifiers take precedence over spatial sensibilities, in his opinion. While I acknowledge his perspective as a designer, it is both problematic and tricky to come up with assured opinions of lived experiences that might be so thoroughly removed from one's own.

This revivalism, I fear, unavoidably leads to a degree of fetishism. It is also, after all, a type of furniture. How far then do you remove an object from its context in an attempt to revive it? The stainless-steel charpai by Alex Davis on display at the exhibition was thus beguiling for many viewers, including myself. The accompanying note reads: "... made of 304 grade stainless steel [it] can be used both indoors and outdoors." If one of the intentions is a serious attempt to preserve and distribute the know-how of charpai-making, what role does this particular piece play? For me, it came off as a rather frivolous addition that was at odds with the rest of the show's sentiments. At this point, it is useful to go beyond the confines of the Adil Shah Palace, and consider on a larger scale what many high-end design boutiques and independent designers have been doing with their time (and in most cases, extensive resources). For example, a Sydney-based designer[7] is selling charpais for 990 Australian dollars, which is close to 50,000 Indian rupees in value. The Attic, a Dubai-based furniture store, lists "charpai benches" for 550 dirhams, or over 10,000 Indian rupees.

More such examples can be found. Does an undertaking in preserving such generational knowledge also charge us with the responsibility to take issue when developed countries continue to shop for non-copyrighted knowledge, as if they are items waiting to be picked up from an interdisciplinary shopping aisle? The ethical apprehensions around taking that which is in the safekeeping of marginalised groups, while these groups themselves fail to gain benefits as stake-holders, is an important aspect of differentiating inclusivity from appropriation. Given this background, what are the moral obligations of selling charpais when the differential between the price of a charpai sold in India, the place of its origin— these are available in New Delhi within the range of 800 to 2500 Indian rupees—and Sydney is nearly twenty-fold? Both Kasliwal and Thakker, who was a chief resource person for the exhibition, take a less political view. They are mainly concerned with the targeted market when it comes to the question of ethics. Kasliwal argues that "everybody used to make it, so what is being done isn't being done at the cost of people like Hem Singh (an expert charpai-weaver from Jodhpur and a long-time collaborator of Kasliwal's). They've always done it in [their] context. They've always done it for themselves and they've exchanged it. It doesn't threaten their identity or their livelihoods either. Were they going to work in Sydney? No." He also makes a distinction between this and where he would draw the line at appropriation. If a specific set of motifs that can clearly be identified as belonging to a certain community are abused by mass-production outside of that community, he would find it reproachable. Thakker adds to this stance that buying practices would certainly concern him. Unless these charpais were being bought at low prices locally and resold at exotic rates, he shares the curator's belief that it is noteworthy that the charpai continues to reach new places. Thakker draws attention to another interesting aspect of the charpai: while the basic structure historically remained the same, wealth sometimes dictated how it came to be embellished and which materials were used.

Still, for Kasliwal, the charpai is also a signifier of identity. He sees it as something that belongs to the subcontinent, that is ours, and it is exactly because he sees it as such that he believes its proliferation through boutique design houses and places it may not have been previously used, is a cause for celebration of the charpai's genius. That is why he doesn't regard the removal of the charpai from its social structures, which he considers it so intrinsic to, as a type of erosion. Even if I were to lay aside my reservations about assuming ownership in such broad terms, I'm not entirely convinced that just because a market has the potential for growth, it should be considered an endorsement to be proud of. This poses the question: does endorsement equal relevance?

POLITICKING WITH THE CHARPAI

The bid to commandeer the charpai's relevance is not only in strictly market-driven quarters. Sunaina Kumar draws attention to an Indian National Congress rally in Rudrapur, Uttar Pradesh called by Rahul Gandhi, which attempted to play into the "idea of the mofussil"[8] (or rural areas) by organising a *khaat sabha* involving actual jute and wood charpais. The concept spectacularly backfired: multiple news sources reported that attendees made off with the charpais the Party had sourced. Comedic as it may be, Gandhi isn't the only one to try and tap into the charpai's mass appeal. A photo of Pakistan's Prime Minister Imran Khan sleeping on a charpai, tweeted by the President Arif Alvi, shows a much younger Khan with the caption: "This photo was taken by me from my Charpai when we slept under a hot night sky in Nagarparker, Tharparker sometime around 1997. The road to his premiership has been long [and] hard, however, his passion to serve Pakistan knows no bounds."[9] The messaging is clear enough. At over thirty-three thousand likes, "*charpai pe sona*" as one retweet glibly put it, gave the impression of "simplicity" and being "down to earth." The charpai as the symbol of the man in touch with the people, amusing as it is, does reveal something about where it stands in the public consciousness. Another figure in public office I came across on Twitter trying to capitalise on this was Martin Kobler, the German Ambassador to Pakistan. His tweet read: "Just went to a local shop and bought a charpai for FC guards; was hard to distinguish between the quality. Look at the old one. Who protects us definitely deserves some good sleep. P.s they make some really good naan in that woodoven."[10] This posturing doesn't seem to be based on a reductive view of those it is attempting to impress. Certainly, deploying objects in public spaces as a political token to reassure the voting public that the leader identifies as "onc of us" isn't in itself new, nor is the manner in which mass media propaganda plays a role in creating a mimicry of the working class that the political elite in turn, pretends to identify with. Given the sheer magnitude and the range of such applications, is the measure of this specific set of combinations in its success?

The Charpai Project, prior to its final realisation at Serendipity Arts Festival, included an open call to young designers from CEPT University (Ahmedabad), Pearl Academy (New Delhi), Indian Institute of Crafts and Design (Jaipur), Indian School of Design and Innovation (Bombay), and Creaticity (Pune), following a workshop on charpai weaving. Given a brief that the charpai is "iconic to the country and the subcontinent. As a product it is very frugal, it makes do with very little, you can use it in many different ways and when you move it around, your space changes," designers were invited "to reinvent not just the product, but the technique, the skill, the craft, the idea of sustainability." A section commending the participants and winners was included at the Festival in Panjim as a marker that Kasliwal's project with the charpai is on-going. Apart from the little "shop", Ayush brought in several beautiful charpais made by Hem Singh, sourced during his research trips. Woven into the design of two of these, one a striking red and another in a soft blue, are the dates on

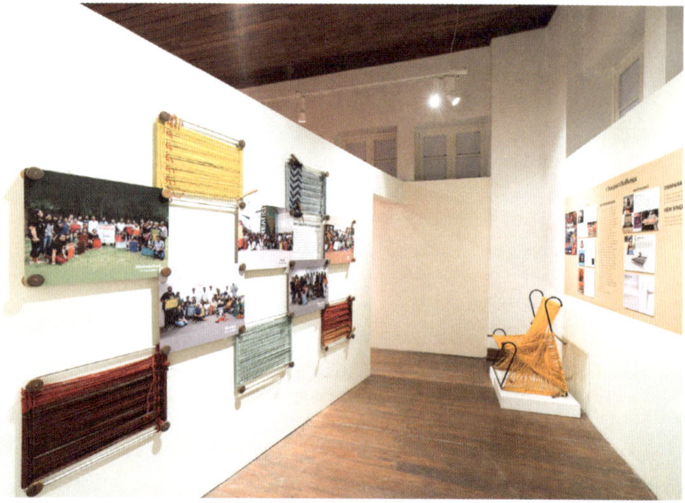

Installation view of *The Charpai* at Adil Shah Palace

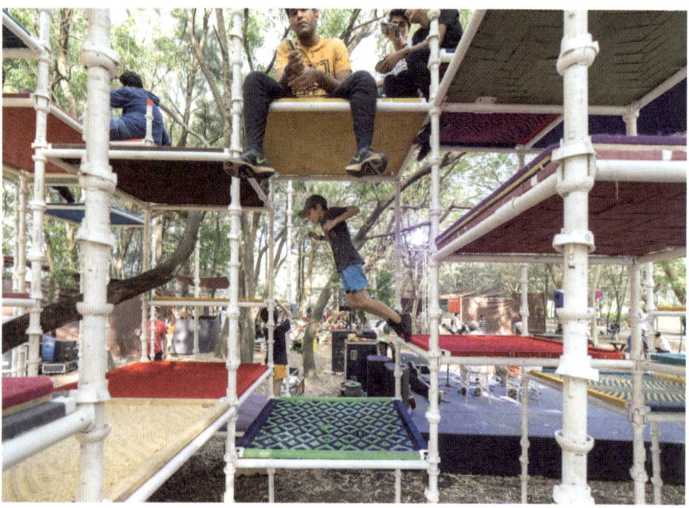

Scenes from *The Charpai* at The Children's (Art) Park

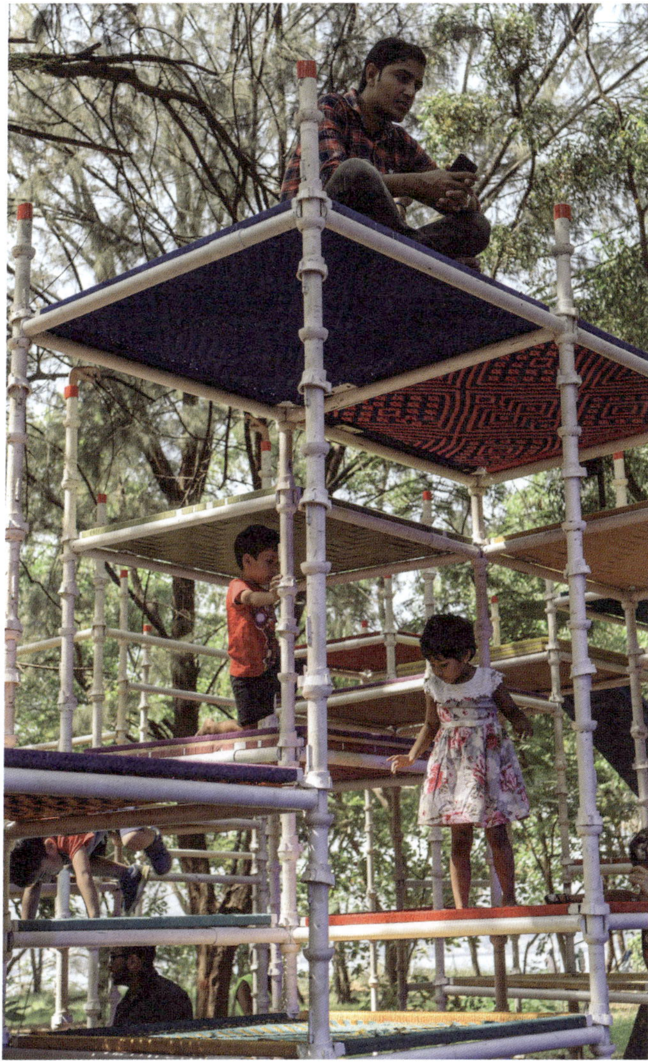

Scenes from *The Charpai* at The Children's (Art) Park

which they were completed. The letters 'HSR' denoting Hem Singh Rathore can also be seen on the red charpai. A collection of charpais and day-beds constructed from a variety of materials (including the rather controversial charpai crafted in stainless steel) grace the opposite side of the wall where miniaturised charpais displaying the many kinds of weaves that are used across different states had been put up. Perhaps between them, they reinforced the curator's stand, that the charpai is fluid in design and ultimately a people's object.

Notes

[1] The phrase "Charpai in Time" is drawn from a sub-title featured in the curatorial note for the project authored by Ayush Kasliwal.

[2] Sunaina Kumar, "Cot in action: A short history of the Indian khaat, from Ibn Battuta to Rahul Gandhi," *Scroll.in*, published online September 8, 2016, https://scroll.in/article/815912/cot-in-action-a-short-history-of-the-indian-khaat-from-ibn-battuta-to-rahul-gandhi.

[3] Kumar, "Cot in action: A short history of the Indian khaat, from Ibn Battuta to Rahul Gandhi."

[4] Mitraja Bais, Ben Cartwright, Samrudha Dixit, Jay Thakkar, *Sahaj: Vernacular Furniture of Gujarat* (Ahmedabad: CEPT University Press, 2018).

[5] Garrett Hardin, "The Tragedy of the Commons," *Science,* New Series 162, no. 3859 (1968):1243.

[6] Hardin, "The Tragedy of the Commons," 1243.

[7] Anurag Verma, "Australian Man Selling Charpoy For $990 Has Left Indians Dumbfounded," *News18*, Updated on October 6, 201, https://www.news18.com/news/buzz/australian-man-selling-traditional-charpoy-for-990-has-left-indians-dumbfounded-1537967.html.

[8] Kumar, "Cot in action: A short history of the Indian khaat, from Ibn Battuta to Rahul Gandhi."

[9] Arif Alvi (@ArifAlvi), Twitter post, August 18, 2018, 10:17 PM, Accessed May 1, 2019.

[10] Martin Kobler (@GermanyinPak), Twitter post, January 4, 2019, 4:05 AM, Accessed May 1, 2019.

Biographies

Senjuti Mukherjee studied Comparative Literature and Arts and Aesthetics at Jadavpur University and Jawaharlal Nehru University respectively. Since 2013, she has catalogued and researched visual arts collections and related archives with organisations such as Osian's, Eka Cultural Resources, and DAG, focussing on film publicity memorabilia, various photographic mediums and processes, and political theatre. At DAG, she has also curated a film programme called Art on Film screening films on and by Indian modern artists. In addition, she has worked closely with several exhibitions of the contemporary arts during her time at Nature Morte.

In the recent years, she has been exploring the material culture of the celluloid medium, cinematic and photographic apparatus, and undergone training in celluloid preservation and conservation at workshops held by the FIAF and Film Heritage Foundation. Recently, she has curated a research module on celluloid film studios and laboratories of erstwhile Madras for Sahapedia's online archive. At Serendipity Arts Foundation, she has served as the Project Head and Editor for Projects/Processes 2018.

Skye Arundhati Thomas is a writer and editor based in Mumbai. She is a contributor writer at artforum, Frieze, e-flux, ArtReview, ArtMonthly and is Contributing Editor at The White Review.

Bharathy Singaravel is a member of the Editorial Collective at the Indian Writers Forum and a freelance writer. She is interested in cultural politics and has written on it for the Indian Cultural

Forum, Newsclick and Umbra - Journal of Film Culture in India. She has worked at the Kiran Nadar Museum of Art as as an Associate Researcher and at Nature Morte as a Gallery Manager.

About Projects/Processes

Projects/Processes is an initiative launched by Serendipity Arts Foundation in 2017 to publish commissioned research essays, longform writing, and in-depth criticism that explore the ideas and processes behind select curatorial projects at Serendipity Arts Festival. Over three years, the Festival has accumulated a rich database of creative energies and partnerships. As an eight-day long event, the Festival is a platform for multidisciplinary collaboration and cultural innovation, and has commissioned over 90 new works across the visual and performing arts since its inception in 2016. The Projects/Processes series offers an opportunity to give some of these works and the stories that they tell continued life, through a deeply engaged look at how they came together and their significance to the discourse of contemporary art in India moving forward. Each volume comprises essays covering distinct projects that stand in some dialogue with each other, through the questions they raise and the thematic landscape they cover.

Project Head & Editor: Senjuti Mukherjee
Managing Editor: Nandita Jaishankar
Copy editors: Arnav Adhikari & Arushi Vats
Cover design and layout: Aman Srivastava

Projects/Processes as an initiative is conceptualised and supported by Mr. S. K. Munjal, Founder Patron, Serendipity Arts Foundation and Ms. Smriti Rajgarhia, Director, Serendipity Arts Foundation.

About Serendipity Arts Festival

Serendipity Arts Festival (SAF) is one of the largest multi-disciplinary arts initiatives in the South Asian region. It spans the visual, performing and culinary arts, whilst exploring genres with film, live arts, literature and fashion. Besides the core content, which is conceptualised by an eminent curatorial panel, the Festival has various layers of programming, in the form of educational initiatives, workshops, special projects, and institutional engagements. Through active conversations between the artistic community and the urban, social landscape, the festival continues to evolve around the mandate of making art visible and accessible. The festival seeks collaborations at its core, inspiring new perspectives of seeing and experiencing. The Festival is a cultural experiment that also addresses issues such as arts education, patronage culture, interdisciplinary discourse, inclusivity and accessibility of the arts.

About Serendipity Arts Foundation

Serendipity Arts Foundation is an organisation that facilitates pluralistic cultural expressions, sparking conversations around the arts across the South Asian region. Committed to innovation and creativity, the aim of the Foundation is to support practice and research in the arts, as well as to promote sustainability and education in the field through a range of cultural and collaborative initiatives. The Foundation hosts projects through the year, which include institutional partnerships with artists and art organisations, educational initiatives, grants and outreach programmes across India.